Published by

Good Word Productions

Providing words of
encouragement and inspiration
through writing and speaking.

*Anxiety in the heart of man
causes depression,
But a good word makes it glad.*

(Proverbs 12:25—NKJV)

Table of Contents
A Month of Love Stories

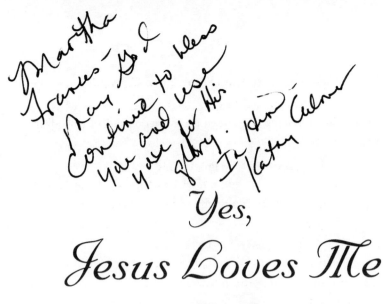

Yes, Jesus Loves Me

31 Love Stories

Edited by

Kathy Hood Culmer

Good Word Productions
Kingwood, Texas
2003

Good Word Productions
P.O. Box 5124
Kingwood, Texas 77325

ISBN Number—0-9715353-0-2
Library of Congress Control Number—2002095842

Permissions

All scripture quotations, unless otherwise indicated, are taken from the HOLY BIBLE, NEW INTERNATIONAL VERSION®, NIV®, Copyright ©1973, 1978, 1984 by International Bible Society. Used by permission of Zondervan. All rights reserved.

Scripture quotations marked "KJV" are taken from the Holy Bible, King James Version, Cambridge, 1769.

Scripture quotations marked "NKJV" are taken from The New King James Version / Thomas Nelson Publishers, Nashville: Thomas Nelson Publishers, Copyright © 1982. Used by permission. All rights reserved.

Scripture quotations marked "NLT" are taken from the Holy Bible, New Living Translation, copyright 1996. Used by permission of Tyndale House Publishers, Inc., Wheaton, Illinois 60189. All rights reserved.

Book Layout & Design—Rita Mills
Cover Design—Gladys Ramirez
Copy Editor—Helen Britton
Line Editor—M.A.S. Stautberg
Book Consulting & Production by The Book Connection
w w w . t h e b o o k c o n n e c t i o n . n e t

The paper used in this publication meets the requirements of the American National Standard for Permanence of Paper for Printed Library Materials Z39.48-1984.

Printed in the United States of America

Dedication

To my loving husband, John, who believed, encouraged and supported me from the start—my love and gratitude always. May this new partnership reap a bountiful harvest.

To my beautiful daughters, Kellee, Courtney, and Candace who listened even when you didn't want to and who asked, "Aren't you done with that yet," which let me know you were really paying attention—may you continue to know and grow in the knowledge of His love for you and ours for you, too.

To my friends and sister-friends who prayed with me and for me on this project, who encouraged me with your words and deeds, who read and listened, and who have just been there for me for so many days and in so many ways—I will always treasure your friendship.

To my sisters-in-Christ who said, "Yes," and have shared your hearts and your stories in this collection—Keep on being a blessing!

To Mur-Callie whose love and prayers continue to bless me. You are in my heart always.

To Him Who made me, saved me, called me, Who loves me anyhow and keeps on blessing me no matter what—to You, O God, be the glory!

Introduction

God loves you! God wants you to know that He loves you—that He always has and that He always will. He wants you to know that nothing can ever separate you from His love. Nothing you do or say or think will ever cause God to stop loving you. When you know this, when you can grasp this truth and let it sink deep down in your soul and take root, you will experience a freedom you have never known. You will find rest in the knowing. You will find peace there. Strength there. Healing there. Once you reach this realization, you will want to spend the rest of your days pleasing the Lover of your soul.

The women whose stories are recounted in this book are sharing the experiences that God allowed in their lives to bring them to the realization that, "Yes, Jesus loves me, Jesus loves even me!" Their stories are the ways in which He planted that truth deeply into their souls. It is a planting that gives life and hope and the promise of eternity, not only to them but to all whose lives they touch. Each of the experiences shared has been a life-changing experience and, in some cases, a life-saving encounter with the Almighty.

Some who have shared their stories have been refreshed by the remembering. Some have been first grieved by the memories, though only for a short while, and then healed by the recalling. Some have journeyed back to pleasant places while others have revisited difficult times, but all have done so willingly and joyously for you. Each of the experiences bears witness to the discovery of a very special love—the love of the Creator, God, for His created—the love of the One who is Himself Love.

Maybe you have already heard His whisper, felt His warm embrace, experienced God's wonderful love for yourself, and maybe these stories will help you to remember your own, then to be renewed and refreshed by the recollection. If not, perhaps God will speak of His love for you through the stories or in some other unexpected way.

For you who do not yet know God's love, my prayer is that you will soon come to know His wonderful, unconditional, undying, life giving and life saving love for yourself. And for us all, my prayer is that we will walk in His love, grow in it, live fruitfully and abundantly in it. Then, with the precious gift of His love, let us do as He has given us charge to do: love others as He has loved us.

—Kathy Hood Culmer

For God so loved the world
that He gave His one and only Son,
that whoever believes in Him
shall not perish but
have eternal life.
(John 3:16)

Foreword

In this day when there is unrest all around us, many may fear and wonder what is going to happen Those that believe in the name of Jesus Christ can walk in His peace. He offers us a peace that surpasses man's understanding. This peace can only come through our trust in Him when we have an understanding of His love for us.

God loves us with an everlasting love—a love that carried His son Jesus to the cross where He gave His life for our iniquities and transgressions, then on the third day He arose and ascended into heaven with all power. There, he makes intercession for us because he is the sacrifice for our sins—and not for ours only, but also for the sins of the whole world. Jesus is our High Priest and our advocate. He has been touched with the feeling of our infirmities; He was in all points tempted just as we are, yet is without sin. He offers forgiveness of sin to us in 1 John 1:9 which says, "If we confess our sins, He is faithful and just to forgive us our sins, and to cleanse us from all unrighteousness."

The cross represents the completeness of the love of God for us through Jesus. Jesus demonstrates His love toward us daily in real and practical ways. His love manifests itself through us when we love one another as ourselves. We apply that love daily by being kind one to another in word and deed, tenderhearted, forgiving one another; acting for the welfare of those taxing our patience; encouraging one another; admonishing one another in love; helping one another in times of need; rejoicing with one another in times of joy; exalting others more highly than ourselves. It is in the everyday experiences of our lives that He makes His love known both to us and through us. When we love one another as ourselves, then we know we have the love of Christ in us and His love flows through us. Jesus says if we have this, we are children of the light, and He lives in us.

Everyone will not have a Damascus Road experience as did the Apostle Paul; everyone will not recognize a wilderness experience as did Jesus; everyone will not have a supernatural experience as did Moses, but everyone will have encounters with Jesus through people and circumstances. So, let us be content with the word of God that tells us He loved the world so much that He gave His son for us, and ask Him to bring us into the revealed knowledge of that love toward us. Let us recognize and seek to understand the love of Jesus that comes to us each day bringing with it opportunities to receive it and demonstrate it before others.

If you do not yet know Jesus Christ as your personal Lord and Savior, get to know Him, He offers life—new life—eternal life through this: *"That if you confess with your mouth the Lord Jesus and believe in your heart that God has raised him from the dead, you will be saved. For with the heart one believes unto righteousness, and with the mouth confession is made unto salvation"* (Romans 10:9-10). Therefore, you can know that "Yes Jesus Loves Me."

—Burnice Marshall

When I consider Your heavens,
the work of Your fingers,
the moon and the stars,
which You have set in place,
what is man that You are mindful of him,
the son of man that You care for him?
You made him a little lower than the heavenly beings
and crowned him with glory and honor.
(Psalms 8:3-5)

Judy Neptune is the
Lay Director of the Deaf Ministry
group of the
Episcopal Diocese of Texas.
She regularly interprets for the
deaf in her parish of
St. John the Divine in Houston
where she is a member of the
Daughters of the King,
a leader of a ChristCare group,
and active in Cursillo.
As well as a past career in nursing,
she has also been a
church organist.
Judy and her husband, Don, are
parents of two grown children
and grandparents of six.

✝

Judy's Love Story

Yes, Jesus loves me. This I truly know! To *know* beyond a doubt that Jesus loves me is an awesome realization. To say that I *know* Jesus loves me suggests that I have a personal and intimate relationship with the Sovereign Lord of the universe. And that is awesome! When I think about it, I cannot help but wonder in amazement as did the Psalmist, *"What is man that You are mindful of him . . . that you care for him?" (Psalms 8:4).* I wonder why God is mindful of me—why and how I matter to Him.

I began to understand many years ago during a trip to the ocean. I had not seen the ocean in several years and I felt I needed to experience the amazing beauty and power of that part of God's creation. In retrospect, I believe that God was then calling me apart from "my world" into a quiet place with Him—that I might find rest—that I might find discovery—that I might comprehend more fully His love and His power.

My husband and I hired babysitters and went to Corpus Christi (The Body of Christ) for a brief time away. We checked into a hotel and stopped in the gift shop where I saw an interesting postcard that described "The Legend of the Crucifix Fish." The story tells how the lowly salicat (salt water catfish) was chosen to bear the marks of a Suffering Savior. One can see the outline of His body on the cross in the backbone of the fish, and there also is the hilt of the sword that was plunged into His side. On the other side of the bone is the clearly discernible imprint of a Roman shield. According to the legend, when you shake the bone of the fish, you can hear the dice that were tossed for our Lord's blood-stained robe. Those who can hear them, it is said, will be blessed.

The next morning we drove to the beach. It was February, so the beaches were not crowded. We parked and began walking down the sandy shore and started looking for shells. As I scanned the shore I saw an object that looked like a fish (the only one on the beach) and walked toward it. I discovered that it was indeed a dead fish that was partially decomposed. I thought about the postcard and wondered if this could be a Crucifix Fish. I knew that I had to find out. So, armed with my cuticle and bandage scissors and nurses' training, I began the delicate surgery.

When my husband saw me busily working over this object, he came to investigate. Of course he was disgusted with my project and tried to dissuade me from this smelly task, but something led me to believe that God had put this dead fish here for me to discover. My husband was further dismayed, er, disgusted when he realized that I was taking the fish back to our hotel room to finish the job. I needed more instruments, like tweezers. On my way back to the room, I stopped at the gift shop and purchased that postcard because I believed I had truly found a *gift* from God.

The end result was worth all the unpleasantness of that quest. I read the postcard to my husband to confirm the gift of love given to us that day from our Lord and Savior, Jesus Christ. We heard the sound of dice rattling when I shook the backbone of the fish, and knew we were truly blessed by His love.

What am I that God is mindful of me—that He would love me so—but to put a smelly ol' fish on the beach, a fish that held the visual reminders of what He did out of love, just for me?

P. S.—Twenty years later on the Galveston Beach, God re-affirmed His love. From down the beach I heard my husband say, "Oh no, not again!"

How great is the love
the Father has lavished on us,
that we should be called children of God!
And that is what we are!
(1 John 3:1)

LaVerne Adams, M. Div.,
is the Senior Pastor of the
Cathedral of Praise Community Church
located in West Philadelphia.
She is also the Executive Director
of the church's
Community Outreach Ministry
which daily operates the
Motivational Achievement Program
(M.A.P.), a before and after school program
for approximately 100 children.
Rev. Adams' passion is her church and
community but travels
across the country preaching
and teaching God's Word.
She was born in Brooklyn, NY
where she met and married
her husband of 20 years, Bruce.
They have two children and
reside in the suburbs
of Philadelphia.

✝

LaVerne's Love Story

"Yes, Jesus loves me. Yes, Jesus loves me.
*Yes, Jesus loves me . . .."** *

Sitting on the floor in a closet in our small apartment, I remember talking to God. I was about six years old asking God some very complex questions. Why did things have to be so hard? With my mother and six sisters living in a one-bedroom apartment, things were always tight and hard. I remember that on one particular occasion, I was angry. There had just been some silly conflict—again. I hated conflict. I avoided it like the plague. I wanted us to all get along. But that seemed impossible in such close quarters. I had reached a level of unmanageable frustration.

I remember that on the floor of a closet, this little girl poured her heart out to God. I told God everything the best I could, and I asked for His help. And somehow, I knew that God heard me. As I cried out to Him, I felt my frustration subsiding, and I began to feel an overwhelming sense of love. Though I did not know it then, years later I would have to say that that was the beginning of my love-relationship with God. *"He that cometh to God must believe that he is and that he is a rewarder of them that diligently seek him"* *(Hebrews 11:6).*

Funny thing is, I don't even know how I knew that I could go to God, that I could cry out to Him, or that I would be heard by Him. We were not church-goers; so I hadn't even learned about Him in Sunday School like some of my classmates at the nearby parochial school that I attended on a benevolence scholarship. It was there at St. Gregory's School that I first learned that God existed and that there were angels. Just before His crucifixion, Jesus said to His disciples, *"You did not choose me, but I chose you . . ."* *(John 15:16).* Could it have been that God had chosen me?

Ms. Dorica was my teacher at St. Gregory's, and she was so sweet. I never knew sweetness such as hers. Her kindness and attention were in direct contrast to everything I had ever experienced. Maybe it was the way that she looked at me and really "saw" me. Or maybe it was the softness in her voice when she spoke to me and the other children. Or perhaps it was the way that she encouraged me with her nurturing words. Whatever it was, at those moments when I was in her presence, I felt special. I felt God's love.

Ms. Dorica must have been my own personal angel sent by God. She demonstrated the love of God in a way that has made such a lasting impact on my life. She brought out the best in me. I performed for her and was an excellent student. The impact that her warmth, her compassion, and her "softness" had on me continues to shape my life and ministry. The outreach ministry of the church where I now pastor centers around the love and care of children. Most of our children come from single-parent homes, as I had come. Part of the goal of this ministry is to provide to these children a kind word, or a soft touch, or to add a bit of sweetness to their little lives in the hope that theirs might be transformed as mine had been. *"Suffer the little children to come unto me, and forbid them not: for such is the kingdom of God"* (Mark 10:14).

When I was a girl, my mother had to work two and three jobs outside the home just to make ends meet. And although I missed her and loved her and did not always understand, I found my peace in knowing that I had God. This God, whom I came to know as My Heavenly Father, would come to me in the quiet. He would come to me in my loneliness. He would hear me every time I called.

Since my mom's retirement, the time I missed with her as a child has been restored to me manifold. *"I will restore twice as much to you"* (Zechariah 9:12). She is there to give me all of the love and attention I need. So, too, is my Daddy God there for me through His Son Jesus Christ, just for the calling. *"Thanks be to God, which giveth us the victory through our Lord Jesus Christ"* (1 Corinthians 15:57).

"Yes, Jesus loves me. Yes, Jesus really loves me. Yes, Jesus loves me, for in so many ways, He tells me so."

---

* *Jesus Loves Me,* Traditional. Words by Anna B. Warner, 1860.

Come to me, all you who are weary and burdened,
and I will give you rest.
Take My yoke upon you and learn from me,
for I am gentle and humble in heart,
and you will find rest for your souls.
(Matthew 11:28-29)

Lessie Washington Harvey
attended
Houston Bible Institute,
currently the
College of Biblical Studies,
in the early 80's.
She then founded the
Ladies Outreach Mission
that ministered to women
in her community through
prayer, Bible study, videos, and retreats.
Lessie has spoken at retreats,
led prayer groups,
taught church groups,
and facilitated small
group Bible studies.

✝

Lessie's Love Story

Yes, I know that God loves me, but recalling just the experience that brought me into that knowledge, or defining just that exact moment in time when I came to know that He loves me, I cannot do. In fact, it's taken me years to truly understand that He loves me, at all. Knowing that He loved others, that was easy to comprehend. After all, I could see His love for others in the "good things" that happened to them or in the protection and blessings they received. But, seeing where God loved me personally, or at all, was hard to grasp. To be perfectly honest, I didn't think anyone, God or otherwise, loved me.

Maybe it was because of the many struggles I'd had in my life. There were so many layers that He had to peel away before I would trust Him. Racial discrimination, injustice, personal sin, and relationship problems made it difficult for me to trust a God who supposedly loved everyone. If He was so loving, why didn't He make things right? How could I trust or love a God who saw the difficulty I had in simply getting through the day and who allowed it without doing anything? Would I have found any comfort in His words, "*. . . though now for a little while you may have had to suffer grief in all kinds of trials. These have come so that your faith—of greater worth than gold . . . may be proved genuine*" *(1 Peter 1:6-7)*. I don't know.

Then, I met Him. Unexpectedly, at one of the low periods in my life, He made Himself known to me. But because it wasn't the encounter I imagined it would be, I didn't want to accept it. I wanted God to come face to face with me so I could tell Him all my hurts and concerns. Then He could apologize for allowing me to be hurt and could get on with the business of making everything better.

He showed me myself. Instead of meeting my demands and asking my forgiveness, God brought me face to face with myself. For the first time in my life, I saw myself as I truly was—a sinner. The peeling back of layers had begun. To me I had always been "good," because, well, because, I always compared myself to others who weren't as good as I. But God compared me to Himself. What an ugly image! How unfair of God to make me look at myself in comparison to Him! *"Before him all the nations are as nothing; they are regarded by him as worthless and less than nothing. To whom, then, will you compare God? What image will you compare him to?" (Isaiah 40:17-18)* Being compared to the imperfect, I could deal with, but being measured against perfection was more than I could handle. I could not help wondering, "How could God love me?" Even I didn't love me.

Then, I met His Son. After God had shown me my true self, He showed me something, or should I say, someone else. He began to deal with me regarding His Son, Jesus Christ. God had to know that I wasn't a middle-man kind of person. I didn't believe it was necessary to go through a middle man to reach God. I didn't like dealing with middle men. If I had a problem, I went straight to the top to get the problem resolved. Jesus Christ was unnecessary in my opinion. I also had a problem with the part about Jesus being

Lord of my life. After managing my life, I thought, for so many years, it was hard to believe that someone could do a better job than I.

While I still resisted and tried to hold on to my old way of seeing things, He began to draw me more and more into His Word. God began to teach me through His Word about His Son Jesus. As I learned more of Him, the mistrust began to leave. More layers peeled away. As the mistrust left, I found myself open to receive the wonderful gift of His love—for me—that Jesus Christ loved me enough to die on the cross to set me free from sin.

So, when it happened, I don't really know. Somewhere over the course of time, I realized God loves me. Somewhere in between the getting the focus off myself, the looking more at Jesus and learning more of Him, the reading of the Word and the learning of the truth, the drawing of me to Himself . . . somewhere along the way it happened. When, I'm not sure, but I came to know that He loves me. All layers peeled away, He has taught me to trust Him with my problems as well as my joys. I am confident of this: that He can and will take care of me.

What an awesome, lovable and faithful God I have that He would draw me into His life and truth and love. Yes, He loves me—as doubting, resisting, and self-reliant as I was—He loves even me.

Your love, O Lord, reaches to the heavens,
Your faithfulness to the skies.
Your righteousness is like the mighty mountains,
Your justice like the great deep.
O Lord, You preserve both man and beast.
How priceless is Your unfailing love!
(Psalms 36:5-7)

Patricia Hutchinson
is currently a
Community Health Nurse
with the
Santa Rosa County Department of Health
serving as a school nurse
for ten schools
outside of Pensacola, Florida.
She has been married to Errol for 26 years,
is the mother of three children,
grandmother of three,
and mother-in-law of two.
Pat has been a believer and follower
of Christ since 1982. She is devoted
to knowing Him more each day and
hopes that by doing so,
her love for Christ will intensify
so much that when others see her,
they will see Him.

✝

$Pat's$ $Love$ $Story$

One snowy wintry day while driving on the ice-clad roads in Syracuse, my mind started to wander. As I looked out over that winter wonderland around me, the trees were silver with icicles forming on the branches; everywhere looked exceptionally clean and bright. I thought, "Now, how can anyone deny the existence of God?" For surely, *"The earth is the LORD's, and everything in it, the world, and all who live in it" (Psalms 24:1).* Surely, only God could make such perfection, such beauty as I saw that while driving along that day. I was so overwhelmed by what I saw that I was completely taken away in thought. I started to think about God's love for humankind and how we have taken that love for granted. When I came out of my near-trance-like state, I felt a deep sadness—a deep void. I was really no different from anyone else. I, too, had taken the beauty of God's creation and His love for granted.

I had been exposed to teachings about God at an early age; but for whatever reason, I guess I didn't yet understand the magnitude of His love. I struggled with these thoughts for months, long after that day when creation had called out to me on that icy road. I actually came to feel tormented.

One Sunday morning, I got dressed and found myself in a little Baptist church down the street, searching for the reason for the void—searching to fill it. Maybe that little church would hold answers about God's love for me and about the beauty of His creation. The people at the church were very friendly; they wanted my address and phone number, which I reluctantly gave them, having convinced myself that it couldn't really hurt.

On Wednesday morning of the week that followed, I was busy trying to literally "get my house in order," since I was scheduled to work later that day. In the midst of my getting things in order, I received a phone call from one of the church members. She wanted to know if she could stop by my house later that evening. I said a reluctant, "Yes," to the woman on the phone, just to get her off my back. I feared she would become a nuisance to me if I didn't agree to the visit.

Throughout the day, I became increasingly anxious, again with thoughts of who Jesus really was and whether or not He cared about insignificant little me. Satan was also having fun with me with taunts like, "There is nothing special about you that anyone would care if you lived or you died. Look at all the people who go about their everyday lives not giving any regard to this God, yet they prosper and seem to be fine." My mind was in turmoil. I didn't know what to believe. I was so confused.

The young lady arrived and was very pleasant. We spoke about child rearing and how difficult it can be at times; then she asked me a very simple question, "If you died tonight, do you know where you would spend eternity?" I had never thought of eternity and where I would spend it. I pondered her question for a while and finally answered, "Well, I don't think I am good enough to go to heaven, and I don't think Jesus even cares about me. I am really a nobody." She then shared some scripture with me from Psalm 139, a passage which has come to be among my favorites:

> *O LORD, you have searched me and you know me*
> *. . . you have laid your hand upon me. Such knowl-*
> *edge is too wonderful for me, too lofty for me to*
> *attain. If I go up to the heavens, you are there; if I*
> *make my bed in the depths, you are there. If I rise*
> *on the wings of the dawn, if I settle on the far side of*
> *the sea, even there your hand will guide me, your*
> *right hand will hold me fast . . . For you created my*
> *inmost being; you knit me together in my mother's*
> *womb. I praise you because I am fearfully and won-*
> *derfully made; your works are wonderful, I know*
> *that full well.*

After reading that passage over and over by myself, it became clear to me that I am important to God, and that, yes, Jesus does love me. Now, I can fully appreciate the beauty of His creation. I can feel His love. I can see Him in everything—know He's in everything. That void is gone, for He has filled it in me.

At one time we too were foolish, disobedient, deceived and
enslaved by all kinds of passions and pleasures.
We lived in malice and envy,
being hated and hating one another.
But when the kindness and love of God our Savior appeared,
He saved us,
not because of righteous things we had done,
but because of His mercy.
(Titus 3:3-5)

Constance Roberts Kelley
is the widow of Henry
who passed away in June of 2001,
the mother of two daughters
and grandmother of six.
Connie is an active member of
Nazarene Missionary Baptist Church
in Evansville, IN where she is
a Sunday School teacher,
member of the Gospel Choir and
serves on the church staff
as a Counselor/Advisor.
In this ministry she assists the pastor
in counseling women and children
of the church and community.

†

Connie's Love Story

"You will seek me and find me when you seek me with all your heart" (Jeremiah 29:13).

I was a young, married woman with two daughters. My husband and I were very involved in the social scene of our community. We were in two social clubs, which afforded us the pleasure and obligations which are the result of a steady flow of friends and invitations to parties and dances. All of this consumed much of our time.

My husband was not attending church at the time, but I was a teacher for a primary Sunday School class at Nazarene Baptist Church. While studying the Bible to teach this class, somewhere along the way, I felt the Holy Spirit beginning to convict me of the double life I was living. I was teaching one thing, but living another. I tried to ignore the tugging of the Spirit, because it meant I would have to make some changes, and I wasn't ready or willing to do that.

I began to pray and ask God to show me what to do and how to do it. After struggling with this feeling for a year or more, I told my husband I was going to have to get out of the clubs because I wanted to get closer to Christ. He was furious—to put it mildly—because, he said that if I got out, then he would have to do the same since they were couples clubs. He made it clear that he wasn't about to stop and that I could just do what I had to do! Needless to say, our marriage was VERY rocky after that. He did his thing, and I did mine—most of the time, not together.

I call that experience my "Moses experience," where I wandered in the wilderness for two years or more. The relationship with my friends was broken—no phone calls—no more invitations—no close relationship with my husband. Ironically enough, this was the time that I came into the full knowledge of Jesus Christ and His love for me. I was so lonely that all I did was study the Bible, pray, and listen to God speak to me through His Holy Word.

> *Bring joy to your servant, for to you, O Lord, I lift up my soul. You are forgiving and good, O Lord, abounding in love to all who call to you. Hear my prayer, O LORD; listen to my cry for mercy.*
> *(Psalms 86:4-6)*

But, that was exactly where God wanted me, with my attention focused on Him and His perfect love for me—as well as for my husband.

God's Word began to change me. It changed the way I looked at my husband and everything else around me. Our children were God's gifts to us, and they were probably the main reason neither of us ever filed for D–I–V–O–R–C–E. I began to change my mode of praying and began asking God to heal our marriage and our hearts. I asked God to bring my husband into a personal relationship with Christ. God taught me to take my eyes off my husband, Henry, and the friends I'd lost—were they true friends?—and look to Him as the example for my life.

As I truly surrendered to God and His Will for my life, everything around me began to change. How I began to see the manifestation of His love! My husband stopped drinking, gambling, staying out late, and whatever else he had been doing. He began staying home and spending more time with me and the children. He expressed that he saw a change in me and my attitude towards him; he felt that something had happened in my life. Praise God!! Something had happened in my life.

My husband rededicated his life to Christ and joined me at Nazarene Church with all the energy he had displayed in the world. I can't express how God opened doors, windows, gates, everything in my life. In my work, in my home, and in my spiritual life, I was overwhelmed at His power, His grace and mercy, as well as His provision for my family.

God's Spirit worked in my life and is still working, changing and correcting through His Word.

And I remain *"confident of this, that he who began a good work in you will carry it on to completion until the day of Christ Jesus" (Philippians 1:6)*. Yes, Jesus Loves Me; I know He does. Jesus loves even me.

But because of His great love for us,
God, who is rich in mercy,
made us alive with Christ
even when we were dead in transgressions . . .
For it is by grace you have been saved, through faith—
and this not from yourselves,
it is the gift of God—
not by works . . .
(Ephesians 2:4-5, 8-9)

Pam Walker
is married and has four children.
She is involved with
community ministry
and has a passion
for women who are hurting.
After being an art instructor
for several years,
she is now a full-time watercolorist.
Her dream is to express
God's word through art.
Pam and her husband Sam
live in Houston, Texas.

✝

Day **6**

Pam's Love Story

∽∽

"Selah"

While touring the new city we'd just moved to after leaving the little farm town that had been our home for the past year, we sat at an intersection on Michigan Avenue in the "big" city of Chicago. It was 5:04 p.m., the end of a workday. As we gazed around, we were surrounded by magnificent skyscrapers and a wave of people pouring out of those monstrous buildings like the opening of a floodgate in a reservoir. We laughed out loud at all of the hustle and bustle created by this circus of people racing to parking lots, running to catch city buses and commuter trains after finishing the day's work. It appeared as though we were looking through a magnifying glass at an ant colony, increased in size 1500 times. This was life in the city at its busiest!

Two years later, and I had become a part of a worker colony of my own making. Though my workplace was not one of those skyscrapers on Michigan Avenue, I had embraced that corporate driven mentality that says busy-ness = success, busy-ness = worthwhileness. I had adopted the mindset that I had to be busy about the Lord's Kingdom doing *things* for Him to be accepted by Him. I had to perform for Him to be rewarded with His love.

Those who knew me would often describe me as being *driven*, or would compare me with the Martha of the New Testament Book of Luke who, when Jesus visited their home, *"was busy with all the work that had to be done,"* while her sister Mary sat at His feet listening to Him teach. Thinking that I had to earn it, I had never accepted God's unconditional love, although it was always there for me. *"For it is by grace that you have been saved, through faith—and this not from yourselves, it is the gift of God—not by works, so that no one can boast" (Ephesians 2:8-9).* Nor did I really understand *all* that was given freely for me on the cross, even though I thought I did. For years, I was as busy as an ant in a colony, making sure I was a good Christian. If there was an avenue to assist in the church or the community, I hopped to it. I read a few Bible verses here and there; I eventually read the entire Bible, seeking favor, perhaps, above understanding. I encouraged others. I was kind and considerate. I prayed prayers.

Many mornings, however, I would awake and feel incomplete. I didn't know why. Deep inside there was emptiness and longing. I wanted to be filled. I longed to know the King of the kingdom. I began to pray for a change in my life. More than anything, I wanted to know that God loved me and accepted me just the way I was, without having to perform.

Years passed, and my family and I made another move. This time the move was to a small town. It was the middle of the summer, and everything was green and growing and in full bloom, unlike the concrete and asphalt we'd left behind. There was no hustle and bustle in this place; instead, everything seemed to move at a snail's pace. And with that move, came new insight. It was as though I was miraculously healed from blindness. Creation looked so different in this place. The flowers all seemed to sing. The trees had a message. The colors in the sky were brilliant. They were all saying, "Selah," which means pause and think on these things. As I marveled at God's creation, I worshipped him for what He had made. Perhaps, it was the first time I experienced true worship. God, not man, had made all that beauty that surrounded me, that called out to me, that touched something deep inside of me . . . and it was all free of effort. It had cost me no more than to look around me and to realize the Creator. No work, no effort had brought me to this realization—only the Creator God, Himself.

As I worshipped Him, I began to feel His love. As I felt His love, I felt, too, His acceptance. Through acceptance, I learned of his Grace. His grace was sufficient and still is, through eternity. I learned, like Mary, to sit at His feet, worship Him, and listen for His voice. *"But one thing is needful: and Mary hath chosen that good part, which shall not be taken away from her"* (Luke 10:42).

Contrary to what I'd thought, I had not found the love and acceptance I'd longed for in the busy-ness; I had not found it in the "doing" for God. I had found it in the quiet. On second thought, I had not found it at all. It had found me. God had called out to me through creation, and I had responded in worship. And now I know for certain that, "Yes, Jesus loves me." He always did and always will.

And I pray that you,
being rooted and established in love,
may have power,
together with all the saints,
to grasp how wide and long and
high and deep is the love of Christ,
and to know this love
that surpasses knowledge—
that you may be filled to the measure
of all the fullness of God.
(Ephesians 3:17-19)

Glenice Robinson-Como
was born in Petersburg, VA
and now resides in
Missouri City, Texas
with her husband, Paul L.,
son, Paul R. and
step-daughter, Dominique,
a student at Arizona State University.
Glenice, who was raised in the
Baptist Church, is now a Postulant
for Holy Orders in the
Episcopal Church in the
Diocese of Texas.

✝

Glenice's Love Story

~≈~

My journey into the knowledge of God's love for me started in the Baptist Church where I grew up. It was there that I came to know the words to the song, "Jesus Loves Me," in the Children's Choir. The phrase was reinforced by our minister and by the little ladies who, Sunday after Sunday, sat in the same seat on the front row of the church. As a child, I called them the "Thank-You-Jesus Ladies," because they were always thanking Jesus for something different each Sunday. They experienced great emotions during the service which would eventually lead to many of them rising to their feet, without their canes or walkers, and boldly confessing the love of God. I always longed to know what could cause a person to feel that type of emotion—what was it that caused their frail bodies to respond so strongly? I once asked a very spirit-filled friend, "How do you experience that type of emotion about God?" Her response to me was simply, "Search your heart." She told me that God resided inside of me. I was still too "green" to even comprehend what she was saying.

It has been a long road leading me from the Children's Choir and the "Thank-You-Jesus Ladies" into the understanding of the simplistic beauty of God's love and mercy towards me. Not until my family relocated to Houston, Texas, did that beautiful love story finally unfold. While visiting an Episcopal Church with a family friend, I heard a sermon which changed the way I viewed the life of our Lord and Savior and the love of God. The message of the day centered on discovering the solutions to all of our problems through Christ. The sermon ended with the priest pointing to the cross on the altar and saying four simple words, "Look to the Cross." As I looked at the Cross, for the first time I saw it all—I saw the nails in Christ's hands for what they really were—piercing and painful. I saw the humiliation, the mockery, the scars, and the blood. It was then that I fully understood what an incredible price had been paid for my salvation. *"For God so loved the world that he gave his one and only Son, that whoever believes in him shall not perish but have eternal life"* *(John 3:16)*. It was then that I knew just how much God really loved me. God so loved *me,* that He gave His Son for my life. With that insight came the painful realization that I had not given God his kudos, that I'd been too matter-of-fact about this great gift. His gift of agape love, His unconditional love for me, was something that I could not and would not ever take for granted again. I began to pray for God's direction and for *His* plan for me. I also prayed for my heart to be changed in order to receive the fullness of His love and to grow in His Spirit.

There is a beautiful children's story called, "Mama, Do You Love Me?" by Barbara Joose*. It is a story that I think I enjoy as much as my son. The story takes place in Alaska and describes a daughter's attempts to define the limits of her mother's love. She asks, "Mama, do you love me? How much do you love me?" Her mother tries to explain to her in terms that a child would understand and replies, "I love you as much as the raven loves his treasure, more than the dog loves his tail, more than the whale loves his

Yes, Jesus Loves Me

spout." The daughter continues to question her mother with all possible situations that would cause displeasure such as, "What if I put salmon in your parka or ermine in your mukluks, would you *still* love me?" Finally, her mother says, "I may be sad, worried, or even angry, but I will love you forever and for always, because you are my dear one." That is what He spoke to me that day as I gazed at the Cross. Though your actions may grieve me or anger me, "I will love you forever and for always, because you are my dear one." That is what God is saying to each of us. He wants us to know that regardless of the mistakes we make in life, His love will sustain us. He wants us to bring all of our flaws and imperfections to Him, because He loves us. God only requires that we confess when we sin; *"If we confess our sins, he is faithful and just and will forgive us our sins and purify us from all unrighteousness" (1 John 1:9)*; that we ask for forgiveness, and that we continually seek Him in our lives. He wants to take all of our broken pieces to form a masterpiece that is only possible through Him.

As I continue on my journey as a Christian, I am learning that there is nothing that can separate us from the love of God, *". . . neither death nor life, neither angels nor demons, neither the present nor the future, nor any powers, neither height nor depth, nor anything else in all creation, will be able to separate us from the love of God that is in Christ Jesus our Lord" (Romans 8:38-39)*. Nothing can separate me from His love. Now, I not only understand the "Thank-You-Jesus Ladies," but I guess you could say I have become one of them. I understand their gratefulness for all of the wonderful blessings they received from God. These days, you can find me at my kitchen sink, or in my car, or even on the phone with a friend, with one hand raised in the air, giving God the glory that He so rightly deserves.

---

*   Barbara M. Joose, *Mama, Do You Love Me?* (San Francisco: Chronicle Books, 1991).

He tends His flock like a shepherd:
He gathers the lambs in His arms
and carries them close to His heart
(Isaiah 40:11)

Dorcas Maxine Brown Colvard
is the sixth of eight children born to
A.J. and Melvina Norfus Brown.
The love of God
that was instilled in her at an early age
continues to guide her
through the ups and downs of life.
Dorcas is married to Robert,
and they have two daughters,
Bridget and Amberr.
She is a member of
Faith United Methodist Church
in Griffin, GA
where she serves as
Worship Chairperson
and teaches Sunday School.

✝

Maxine's Love Story

There is evidence of God's love all around—in the many gifts that He gives—in the experiences that He allows—even in His opening my eyes to see it in what surrounds me. *"You will seek me and find me when you seek me with all your heart (Jeremiah 29:13).*

God's love for me was first revealed, perhaps, through my mother, or the woman who came to be my mother. When my birth mother died, there were eight children left in my father's care. When our father remarried, God saw to it that our second mother was grounded and rooted deeply in Him. She loved us and blessed us as though she had birthed us. In word and in deed, she shared a love with us that can only come from God. His love is like that mother-love that we come to know as children. It comforts. It consoles. It rocks you to sleep, wipes away your tears, lifts you up when you've fallen, dusts your seat off and sends you out into the world again—renewed. And He assures us that *"As a mother comforts her child, so will I comfort you"* (Isaiah 66:13).

Since those growing up days in my mother and father's

household, somewhere along the way, I remember praying and asking God to let me walk in the path with His children. He has answered that prayer many times over. He has blessed me tremendously with godly friends, sister-friends, and sisters, who delight in Him. I feel His love in the God-talk and the girl-talk that we share. I feel God's love in the time that we share and the company we keep. It is a chance to know and experience God's love through others.

As I venture out into this vast world of God's, I'm amazed at the evidence of God's love, not just for humankind, but for all of His creation, His perfect design for everything that He has made. *"Consider the ravens" (Luke 12:24). "Consider the lilies how they grow" (Luke 12:27). "God clothes the grass" (Luke12:28)*.

I'm reminded of God's love for me anytime I'm feeling lost, depressed, sad, unloved, or removed from the presence of God. *"You will keep him in perfect peace whose mind is stayed on You" (Isaiah 26:3)*.

As I study the word of God and become more intimate with Him, He reminds me over and over that His love is unconditional, *"While we were sinners, Christ died for us" (Romans 5:8)*; that *"His love is there, not that I love Him, but that He loved me first" (1 John 4:19)*.

God's love for me is revealed when my little "grand-darlings" call me, "Grandma Maxine." These children have adopted me as another grandmother. It warms my heart to be in their presence.

Many years before I realized God's love for me, He planted Romans 8:28 deep in my heart, *"And we know that in all things God works for the good of those who love him, who have been called according to his purpose."* Before I could even quote it word for word, it was embedded deep in my spirit. Whenever things didn't go the way I felt they should, I knew then, as I know now, that no matter what, God is working things together for good. It was like a lifetime insurance policy that assured me no matter what happened, there would be His love to cover me, 'cause He was working it all for my good.

Yes, Jesus loves me. The reminders are there all around: in His Word, *"For God so loved the world, that He gave His only begotten son, that whosoever believes in him shall not perish, but have everlasting life"* (John 3:16); in His creation; in the relationships; in His provision, *"God has not given us a spirit of fear, but of love, power, and a sound mind"* (2 Timothy 1:7).

Even as I step inside my kitchen door and glance at a magnet that says, "The task before you is never as great as the power behind you," I'm reminded again, "Yes, Jesus loves me."

But now, this is what the LORD says—
He who created you, O Jacob,
He who formed you, O Israel:
"Fear not, for I have redeemed you;
I have summoned you by name; you are mine."
(Isaiah 43:1)

Burnice Johnson Marshall
lives with her husband, Rayford,
and their family in Humble, Texas.
She is the mother of six children
and grandmother of seven.
Burnice is co-owner
with her husband of
Marshall Engineering Corporation.
She is an active member of
Mt. Zion Bible Fellowship Church
where she serves as
The Women's Ministry Coordinator
and is continually involved with
community service.

✝

Burnice's Love Story

〜〜〜

"My Struggle for Growth . . ."

In my father's house, we attended church regularly. It was a Christian-based home. I was baptized at the age of ten, and, even then, I felt a connectedness to God. As a child growing up, and throughout my young adult life, I had a sense of knowing God, but something always seemed to be missing. It was as if God was just out of my reach concerning a personal relationship with Him. The emptiness lingered; my longing increased. By the time I was married and had my first child, I knew that God had to become alive and operative in my life.

My struggle to know God in a deeper way began with a struggle to know myself, just after my first child was born. It was then that I began to experience an intense battle between my perception of who I was, versus who I really was. I saw myself as an educated career woman (it was what I desired; it was what I had prepared for), but now I had been cast into the role of wife and mother. Motherhood, thus, posed a particular dilemma for me. I wanted, without a doubt, to be a good mother. I prayed daily to become one, but there was so much else I wanted to do, as well. I didn't like feeling "out of control" in that area, a feeling which triggered insecurties in other areas of my life.

God delivered me through this period of internal strife, this period of isolation, of guilt-feeling, of wanting to be a good mother and not knowing how. He delivered me through this period of blaming…everybody and everything, especially my husband. After all, he was the one who wanted to start a family. His deliverance came through prayer, through remembering that the Lord's mercy had worked in my life before and trusting that He would bring me through again. His deliverance came through my surrender, accepting the Will of God that I should be wife and mother, not a career person at that time. His deliverance came through the constant love and support of my sisters. Because of these things and God's grace and mercy, I was able to weather the storm. Another truth that made me victorious through self-condemnation and other demonic thoughts is that *God loves me.* And all the while, God was delivering me. He was drawing me closer to Himself. One cannot pray persistently, be in constant communication with God and not be "drawn." One cannot be obedient, follow the command of God and not be "drawn." One cannot feel the love, the grace, the mercy, without being drawn closer to Him.

Growth in God is truly a process. That striving to know who I was and who I was in Him was the beginning of my struggle, the beginning of my process. As a result, however, my beliefs and how I saw myself changed. God had begun to fill the emptiness…the longing. It was, however, only the beginning of His work-in-progress in me. There would be other valleys and peaks with which He would challenge me as I desired to have more of Him, to please Him, to do His work. Yet, I go through the valleys and peaks today with a greater peace and understanding of God's love.

One day, some years ago, while driving alone in my car and pregnant with my now 12-year-old son, God spoke to me saying, "Burnice, if you don't come to me, you will surely die." I remember having an overwhelming fear of the Lord and, at the same time, wanting to know what the statement meant? Did it mean I would die physically or spiritually? Then I realized, it did not matter which, because either death meant separation from God. *"For if you live according to the sinful nature, you will die; but if by the Spirit you put to death the misdeeds of the body, you will live" (Romans.8:13).* I could not bear the thought of separation of any kind from God's love.

As I look back on that experience, I can truly say it was then that I received my confirmation that, *"Yes, Jesus loves me."* That day Jesus offered me life, real life, more abundant life in Him. *"I have come that they might have life, and that they might have it more abundantly" (John 10:10 — NKJV).* While I continue to seek the kingdom of God and His righteousness, the Lord constantly reveals more of Himself to me. Through the study of His Word, I begin to hear Him; through the hearing, I begin to get understanding; through the understanding, I begin to obey Him; through the obeying, I begin to serve Him; by serving Him, I have found myself in Him.

I have loved you with an everlasting love;
I have drawn you with loving-kindness . . .
Again you will take up your tambourines
and go out to dance with the joyful.
(Jeremiah 31:3-4)

Linda Williams
is a member of
Zion Missionary Baptist Church in
Evansville, IN.
She is Assistant Superintendent
of the Sunday School
and a teacher. Linda
has over 20 years experience
as an Employment and Training Instructor
offering expertise in
Assessment and Testing,
Job Readiness Training and
all facets of employment and training.
She is married and
has two children.

✝

Day **10**

Linda's Love Story

"To Everything There is a Season"

Everything has its time. Everything has its season. And, for every season, there is a God-ordained reason. I came to know the personal love of Jesus in a very difficult season of my life, a "season of despair," you might call it. It was a season that included *"a time to break down; a time to build up; a time to weep, a time to laugh; a time to mourn, and finally my time to dance; a time to embrace; and a time for peace"* (*Ecclesiastes 3:3,4,5,8*). But through it all, Jesus kept me.

"A time to break down . . . a time to weep." My season began 18 months before the writing of this story. Since that time, my mother was diagnosed with and has recovered from breast cancer; my brother had open heart surgery; my dad became ill with heart disease; my step-daughter was incarcerated; my sister (who is a nurse) became suddenly ill after returning from a foreign mission trip.

"A time to mourn . . . " My sister-in-law was diagnosed

with colon cancer; my brother-in-law was admitted to a nursing home, speechless and suffering from diabetes, which resulted in his leg being amputated. He had numerous strokes, and before I could finish penning my story, he died.

"A time to embrace . . . " I have, on many occasions, heard that you're either "in a storm, coming out of a storm, or going into a storm." For me, it became a living reality. It seems as though for that 18-month period, however, that I was simply in the storm, not heading towards, not coming from, but stuck there in the middle of a raging storm. As I felt myself drowning, gasping for air, I cried out to God and said, "I need Thee, Oh, I need Thee. I need you, Jesus. I'm just a broken vessel, and I need you to put me back together again." In what seemed my darkest hour, He heard my cry and lifted me out of my despair. Jesus rocked me in the cradle of His Love. He protected me, and He kept me in the midst of it all.

"A time to build up . . . " I have attended church all my life—studied, prayed, fellowshipped with the Saints—but it wasn't until I had gone through this succession of heartbreaking events that I began to feel His love, to really know Him, to really feel like His child. I came to Jesus, weary, worn, and sad. I found in Him a resting place, and He has made me whole. The songwriter says that we all fall down, but what distinguishes the saint from the sinner is that after we . . . those who are called saints . . . those who are called His children, after we fall, we get up.* We get up on His wings and by His grace, and we are made stronger. We are made more usable to Him. We, then, may bring up others with us.

"A time to laugh . . . " Through all that hurting and healing, I knew Jesus loved me, when He wiped all my tears away. He mended my broken heart. He was my:

Rock that is higher than I (Psalms 61:2)
My Shield (Psalms 84:11)
My lamp in darkness (2 Samuel 22:29)

Yes, Jesus Loves Me

My strength and power (2 Samuel 22:33)
My Deliverer and my High Tower (Psalms 18:2)

And, He let me know that the God that I serve *"fainteth not, neither is weary" (Isaiah 40:28).*

"A time for peace . . . " Jesus kept me in perfect peace. God assured me that, *"Weeping may endure for a night, but joy comes in the morning" (Psalms 30:5).* My morning has come, and I have experienced unspeakable joy and a peace that "surpasses all understanding," because of His deliverance and because of His great love for me.

"A time to dance . . . " My family circumstances became so overwhelming that all I could do was STAND. As the same songwriter says in another song, "When you've done all you can do . . . you just STAND."** Let's say that I'm not just standing on the promises of Jesus, but I am ready to dance because of His faithfulness to those promises. He promised never to leave me alone, and He's never left me *(Matthew 28:20).* When I needed Him most, He sent the Comforter to comfort me. His grace and mercy reassure me of His unconditional love. There is no greater love. And because of these things rendered unto me in this, "my season of despair," I do as stated in James 1:2, *"Count it all joy when you fall into various trials,"* confident that He is molding and shaping me to perfection.

I know Jesus loves me because I have a personal, intimate relationship with Him, and He has shown me,

"To everything there is a season."

---

* Donnie McClurkin, *We Fall Down,* Live in London and More, Verity, August 22, 2000.
** Donnie McClurkin, *Stand,* Warner Brothers, October 22, 1996.

Be strong and courageous.
Do not be afraid or terrified . . .
for the Lord your God goes with you;
He will never leave you nor forsake you.
(Deuteronomy 31:6)

Emily Ettling
is a graduate of
Radcliffe College in Cambridge, MA
and Union Theological Seminary
in New York City
where she met her husband, Albert,
to whom she has been married
for 60 years this year.
"I found my faith in college
when I sang Bach's *St. Matthew's Passion*
in our Choral Society," Emily says.
"Blessings have enriched my past;
blessings grace my present,
and blessings will lead me safely
through this life's end."
Emily is currently a member of the
Society of the Companions
of the Holy Cross,
devoted to intercessory
prayer and justice.

✝

Day 11

Emily's Love Story

"My beloved is mine, and I am His." *(Song of Songs 2:16).*

I had my first inkling of what this might mean many years ago. It was my very first experience of God's loving presence and reassuring touch at the time. The beloved memory is as fresh as if it had happened recently, rather than some 60 years ago. It was my first reception of the reality of that unending, supporting love God has for His children.

My faith was born in my freshman year in college when our Choral Society sang Bach's *St. Matthew's Passion* with the Boston Symphony Orchestra. As a result, I became a rarity in the late 1930's among those in my community, someone whose faith was deep and lively. But, it was in my senior year that I had my first true love experience with God.

The college community of which I was a part had no Christmas celebration to enjoy. With my zeal for God and my desire for others to be so inspired, I resolved to create an event to commemorate our Lord's birth. And I did. I planned the service to be held on the Wednesday at twilight just before vacation. I gathered and rehearsed a choir, chose the Bible passages, and even planned the order of the service. I recruited a speaker, our dignified college president, a fairly remote and distant personality. It was to be a candlelight service, and I made those necessary arrangements also.

Everything was ready for the procession on the appointed day as I vested in the proper room. Suddenly, much to my chagrin, I was overcome with fear, even to the point of my knees shaking. With some desperation, I knelt down in the room where I had vested and began to pray. George Washington had worshipped in this church, and a great number of faithful souls had reached out in prayer within those hallowed walls long before I did.

As I knelt there, I had the marvelous experience of feeling the presence of God as I had never known before. It seemed God's hands were placed on my shoulders as I heard the comforting words, "Don't worry, Little One. I am with you and will support you. Go ahead with a confident heart." Paul in his letter to the Philippians from a Roman jail writes, *"Do not be anxious about anything, but in everything by prayer and petition, with thanksgiving, present your requests to God. And the peace of God, which transcends all understanding, will guard your hearts and minds in Christ Jesus"* *(Philippians 4:6-7)*. With a touch and a whisper, He restored to me my confidence and gave me peace. It was the touch of the Master's Hand. It was the embrace of my Beloved.

Over the many years, I have had rich and varied experiences that reassured me of God's love for me personally, but it is this one, my first true love experience, that remains so fresh in my memory that it is as though it happened yesterday.

Since you are precious and honored in my sight,
and because I love you,
I will give men in exchange for you,
and people in exchange for your life.
(Isaiah 43:4)

Mary Blue
has lived in the
Dallas/Ft. Worth, Texas area
since 1999 where she attends
the Potter's House.
She has been married
20 years to a now-retired Army Officer.
They have two daughters and one son.
Mary recently
became a licensed minister.
She has been saved
for 26 years and loves the Lord.
She also loves to read,
bake and sew.

†

Mary B's Love Story

When did I know that God really loved me? Well, I came to know the Lord at age 21, but that was not when. It would be another ten years or more before I came to know of that special love He has for me and me alone.

I came from a single parent home. My dad was an alcoholic and an abusive alcoholic, at that, so my mother split when we were young. Although I was the third child of the six born to this union, I was deemed the most responsible. In fact, there was so much responsibility and so many demands placed on me that I feel I missed out on being a child in many ways.

My dad, whom I had not seen since age nine, died on my 18th birthday. By that time, however, I had gone through two molestations, one of which left me pregnant. With innocence lost and ideals shattered, I began looking for love in all the wrong places. By the time I was 19, I had become, to say the least, promiscuous. From that time to the time of my salvation, I spent two years of living in rebellion, searching for, but never experiencing true happiness.

Then seven years after being saved, I forgave my father for dying on my birthday, for not being a dad to me, and for being the first man to ever put his hands on me. The forgiveness came one Sunday night following an evening service that I'd attended without my family. The message was about forgiveness. I searched myself to see if there was anyone whom I hadn't forgiven who had hurt me or offended me. I thought that I had forgiven all, but the Holy Spirit spoke to me and said, "Now it's time to release your father from that prison in your heart." I could literally envision a little cage full of questions and pain in my heart that was locked so tight I never thought of it or visited it. That night after service, I went to the altar and made a decision to forgive a man who had by then been dead for 15 years. When I forgave him and released him of all the pain he had caused, the Lord opened my heart and filled that empty space with His love.

Two years later I got married and slowly began to develop a friendship with my father-in-law who was not saved at the time. All the while, I was trying to get a handle on God's love for me but was having a hard time and didn't really know why. My father-in-law and I began to sit around after meals and talk while others slept. We would go for ice cream when I was pregnant with my youngest daughter and talk some more. There were so many little things he did to show me I was special to him, but always as a father to his daughter. One day the Lord asked me if I thought my father-in-law loved me. I realized he did. Without ever really knowing my hunger for my own father's love, he was so careful to show me that love. God then said, "Now, imagine how much more I love you than an earthly man who isn't even your natural father." I cried with the understanding that God had used my father-in-law to demonstrate to me the genuine love of a father for his little girl—the love I had so longed for—so long sought after.

I had the wonderful privilege of leading my father-in-law

Yes, Jesus Loves Me

to Christ before he died. I'll always praise God for him because I would have never been able to grasp the love of God without my husband's earthly father showing his love for me! By all accounts of those who knew him, that was quite out of character for him. And that makes me all the more certain that my Heavenly Father orchestrated it all, so that He might give me my heart's desire and so that I might know of His great love for me. I'm so glad He loves me like that!!!

You are forgiving and good, O Lord,
abounding in love to all who call to You.
I will praise you, O Lord my God, with all my heart;
I will glorify Your name forever.
For great is Your love toward me . . .
You have delivered me from the depths of the grave.
(Psalms 86:5, 12-13)

Rose Bostick
is the wife of Michael for 19 years
and mother of two beautiful children,
Niki and Nemo.
Rose has a passion to help others discover
the beauty and practicality
of a relationship with God through prayer.
She strives continually to keep
her relationship to God authentic
and fresh, so that Christ may overflow
in her life to those she serves at home,
as a wife and mother,
at school as an educator,
or just around the neighborhood
as a friend and neighbor.

✝

Rose's Love Story

≈ ≈

"Jesus loves me this I know, for the Bible tells me so,
little ones to Him belong, they are weak but He is strong.
Yes, Jesus loves me . . ."

These simple words, which I have sung so many times as a child and even as an adult, epitomize my faith and the journey of my life. When I look back at the many paths I have taken, some right and some wrong, the rubble and the trouble of my life, whether created or inherited, the prisons of fear and pain endured and conquered, I can clearly see God's hand preserving, sheltering and rescuing me. In the midst of my many efforts to find myself, define and accept myself, just to learn to love myself, I can see the hand of God threaded throughout every sigh, thought and memory, positive and negative, and I am assured of how much Jesus loves me, how much He loves even me.

I was raised in a Christian home. The prayers and songs of my mother filled the spaces with faith and hope and fueled my dreams. The situation in my home, however, was far from ideal, largely because of an abusive father. That, too, influenced my dreams. Although I was saved as a teenager, I did not yet know what it meant to have a relationship with God. I prayed somewhat regularly and read my Bible, largely in part because it was required of me and because I desperately needed God's help to deal with the malfunctions of my life. Such malfunctions included a dysfunctional home, continual health problems, and trying to live and fit into two cultures at the same time. My faith, then, was for the purpose of keeping my sanity and ensuring God's favor upon my future. I believed God was all powerful, but not directly personal. It was only after I married that I realized I really did not know the Lord Jesus, at least not the way my mother knew Him. My mother did not simply *love* Jesus, but she was *in love* with Him. She knew Him in a way that gave her hope in the midst of hopeless situations, namely my father. She didn't just meet Him at church on Sunday. He woke her up and propped her up when she was sick and tired. He dried her tears and brought her comfort. He even assigned angels to protect and give her a report on her children, so it seemed. I wanted to know Him like that.

After the birth of my first child, I experienced post-partum depression, which began what felt like an elevator ride to hell. Pain, plus complications from a Cesarean birth, combined with debilitating migraine headaches that left me temporarily paralyzed, caused that elevator to plummet to a depth of hopelessness, frustration and fear. My inability to function as a new mother and new wife further fueled the depression. I felt then, for the first time in my life, I was in a situation over which I had no control. I tried positive thinking, focusing on positive thoughts of my beautiful baby girl and my husband who loved me and was my knight in shining armor. I thought of my family who was very supportive and resolved to make them my purpose to fight the waves of emotion. After all, the doctors said this should pass in a couple of weeks. And my

Yes, Jesus Loves Me

mother was praying.

A couple of weeks turned into a couple of months. I couldn't take care of my daughter. I couldn't return to my college classes, and the doctors could not find the cause of the headaches. They struck without warning. The medication took care of the pain, but not the paralysis. I could not move limbs, could not speak coherently, and they lasted for what seemed like hours before I drifted into sleep or unconsciousness. I began to lose my hair and had to wear a wig. It was like being in a twilight zone, looking at my worst fears come true. The elevator was plunging rapidly. I kept praying, "God, where are you?" I saw no immediate end to my agony. I kept thinking this was not a future I could handle. I had not survived the struggles of my childhood to end up like this.

One night in the aftermath of another headache and paralysis, I decided I could not handle this anymore. I thought my husband and my daughter would be better off without me. I grabbed my bottle of pills and thought I could just take them all and it would be over. Everyone would think I was asleep, and I would simply never wake up. Then, I looked at my baby girl, who looked like my mother, and I remembered what I had seen my mother endure. I cried out in desperation, "Oh God, I know you as the God of my mother, but I need you to be real to me and rescue me. I can't take this anymore. I'm drowning. Jesus, help me!" I heard a soft voice speak in my mind, "I am here. I will help you. Just trust me. I have been here all along, waiting for you to acknowledge me and seek me. I am the source of your strength and future." I felt a peace come over me that I had never experienced before. I felt the weight of the world lift off my shoulders, and I knew God was real. I recall hearing the words, "This will not end in death. This, too, shall pass." It was then that I felt the power of God's love lifting me to my rescue.

It took a whole year to get out of that elevator of depression and to break the cycle of pain and fear, but God used His Word and people, including doctors to help repair my emotions and restore my health.

The beauty of God's love is that it is transforming. It does not leave you as it finds you. The transformation is a process that takes all of one's experiences, within and outside His will, combined with His truth and grace, to yield a vessel that is fit for the King's appointed purpose and use. I now realize how He used the events of my life to lead me to desire and to seek for what only He could provide, healing and wholeness of the soul. The truth of who Jesus is—the Son of God, my Savior, my Redeemer, and my Provider, my Healer—has transformed my life, and He continues to transform my mind and heart. Each challenge becomes a stepping stone to knowing Him better, loving Him more deeply, and seeing the display of His power in the world around me.

There is nothing more empowering and comforting than knowing the Sovereign Creator God of the Universe cares for me and calls me His child. It was His love that comforted and rescued me that dreadful night, and it is that same love which continues to strengthen and sustain me today. I wish I could say life's road has been easy and I have made no more mistakes since then, but I can't. I don't like elevators, especially after being stuck in one, but I ride them with renewed assurance, faith and hope that they will stop, and the doors will open. I now know whether it moves up or down, God is in control and my destination is in His hands, even when I press the wrong button. Yes, I know Jesus loves me, for He keeps on telling me so.

Because of the Lord's great love,
we are not consumed,
for His compassions never fail.
They are new every morning;
great is your faithfulness.
(Lamentations 3:22-23)

Barbara Garvey
is married and has two daughters.
Barbara has worked
in the community over the years
with the local YMCA,
Girl Scout and Rotary Clubs,
and has served in her church family
as a Sunday School teacher and
member of the Women's Outreach Ministry.
Working in the energy industry
for over 15 years,
Barbara helped to establish
a lunch hour Bible study group.
During that time,
she has seen many lives touched.

✝

Barbara's Love Story

"Lover of My Soul"

At the age of twenty-four, I felt I had seen enough of life from the world's vantage point and dreamed of settling down with the man of my dreams. I recall how we could communicate with each other without uttering a word. He knew my needs without my expressing them, and I knew his. Life was rich and full of promise. Having at last found my soul mate gave me great joy and fulfillment. The greater joy came, however, in knowing that my soon-to-be husband was a Christian and a student of God's Word. We had frequent speaking engagements that allowed us to share with others and bless them as we were blessed.

Yet in the midst of all we shared, the yearning for a family grew. We had purchased what we believed to be our dream home and now longed for the sound of laughter to fill the walls. We had long talks about the broken homes we both came from, and we vowed that our children would never have to suffer what we as children had endured. We would spare our children the heartbreak of an absent parent, of days when money and food were in short supply, and the longing that is sometimes present on long, cold winter nights. With all of this in mind, we prayed fervently for the living God to bless us with a family.

Occupied with furnishing a new home and taking piano lessons, I kept busy, waiting for the manifestation of our dream, while realizing that God works in His own time. After several months passed, I began to feel sick with what I thought was an intestinal virus. I learned, however, from my physician that I was six weeks pregnant. Imagine the joy of knowing that God had answered my prayer and that I was a recipient of His love. Having a saved husband, a new home, and a child on the way, I found life to be wonderful and full of excitement. Six months into the pregnancy, however, I developed edema and had to quit working. Then, as my due date approached, we were faced with other complications. My obstetrician informed me my uterus was not dilating, and I would have to have a C-section to prevent the umbilical cord from strangling the baby. I did, and God blessed us with a beautiful baby daughter.

Three years after giving birth to our first child, I gave birth to our second daughter. Following this birth, however, the relationship between my husband and me became strained. I was preoccupied with the children and had little time for the two of us. He moved out of our bedroom shortly after I came home from the hospital. I thought it was to allow all of us to rest more comfortably during the night and that this would be only a temporary arrangement. The nights rolled into weeks. When I inquired about the existing arrangement, I was told that this was the way it would be. Thinking that this change must have had something to do with the children, and in an effort to salvage our relationship, I arranged for my family to care for the girls for a while. With a hopeful heart, I drove the 300 miles to my mother's and returned the next day eager to begin the recovery process, only to be told by my husband that he would be moving out of the house at the end of the week. At that moment, my hope for the recovery of our marriage vanished, and I became angry. I kept asking him, "Why? What went wrong? What can be done to salvage this relationship? Do the children not matter?"

In just a matter of minutes, all of my dreams were shattered. The hopes I had for a balanced Christian life, an unbroken home, and a loving family for our children had all vanished. I felt abandoned not only by my husband, but by God also. With a high mortgage and a vehicle desperately in need of repairs, my children and I were headed to a homeless shelter, if help did not come. Our children would be destined for the very future we had promised to spare them.

Days later, after an endless flow of tears, I cried out to the Lord as I had never done before. I questioned Him, asking why and how this could happen to me. Since God had blessed me so, I believed I had favor with Him. "Why have you now forsaken me, O Lord?" I cried. The answers that I sought—the peace that I sought—did not come immediately. They did come, thankfully, over the next several weeks from, of all places, my radio. Though my days were filled with the stress of a full-time job, full-time parenting, and the full-time pain of rejection, gradually my nights were bringing me solace. After getting the children settled in for the evenings, I began to listen to the radio broadcast of Dr. Charles Stanley of Atlanta, Georgia. Night after night, there seemed to be a Word from the Lord spoken directly to me through Dr. Stanley's words, ringing down to my ears like "melodies from heaven." In his lessons, he would speak words about exercising faith and trusting in God. I would research the scriptures he would reference and then meditate on the words—truly seeking the lessons of the scriptures for myself. My desire to know more and more about God's truth became unquenchable. The more I heard and read and meditated, the more alive God's Word became in my life. I began to trust God, not my husband, to meet my every need; for *"my God will meet all your needs according to His glorious riches in Christ Jesus"* (Philippians 4:19). Perhaps, for the first time, I believed that He would.

All of this, I know, was by God's loving hand—by His loving design. The seeds that had been planted by Dr. Stanley's teachings—by God's truth—would be put to further test in the days to come. It wasn't long after, that the house—once our dream home—went into foreclosure, and I was faced with the real possibility of becoming homeless. Living on a meager salary and faced with mounting debt, childcare expenses, rent on the house we moved into after being evicted, and the relentless need for car repairs, I was overwhelmed. But through it all, God proved His love and His faithfulness, whether by sending loving people to stand in the gap praying for me and my babies, or by His supplying the thing needed, or by sending a word in due season by Dr. Stanley over the radio. Whatever the need, God supplied it, and because He did, I was not consumed. The *New Living Translation* of Lamentations 3:19-25 sums up the experience:

> *The thought of my suffering and homelessness is bitter beyond words. I will never forget this awful time, as I grieve over my loss. Yet I still dare to hope when I remember this: The unfailing love of the LORD never ends! By his mercies we have been kept from complete destruction. Great is his faithfulness; his mercies begin afresh each day. I say to myself, 'The LORD is my inheritance; therefore, I will hope in him!' The LORD is wonderfully good to those who wait for him and seek him.*

You see, God wants us to rely on Him and Him alone, and He will bring us to just that place of need that causes us to do so.

My walk during the time of my marriage was not based on the relationship I had with God, but on the relationship my husband had with Him, or the relationship I thought he had. I had grown comfortable and accustomed to God's good material gifts, afforded me through my marriage; and, each time a blessing was received, I naturally expected another one. Once God stripped me of those "things"—things that He had given, things that had, perhaps, come to mean more to me than the Giver Himself—I had to stand on God's promises alone of blessing me and restoring the years that the locusts had taken. When I began to walk in the Light, I began to understand how undeserving I was of His grace and mercy and now *"I am overcome with joy because of your unfailing love, for you have seen my troubles, and you care about the anguish of my soul"* (Psalms 37:1, New Living Translation).

Can a mother forget the baby at her breast
and have no compassion on the child she has borne?
Though she may forget,
I will not forget you!
See, I have engraved you on the palms of my hands . . .
(Isaiah 49:15-16)

Demetria Dawkins
is a native of Leland, Mississippi
and currently resides
in Kingwood, Texas. She is from a
household of seven children and
two strong, loving parents where
the importance of education,
family values, God and church
were highly stressed.
"Dee" and her husband, Robert,
have one daughter, Veronica,
who she says has taught her that,
"Patience and waiting on the Lord
is what He needs us to do so we can
fully understand His plan for us."
She is a graduate of
Alcorn State University
and a member of
Zeta Phi Beta Sorority, Inc.

✝

Day 15

Dee's Love Story

⌒⌒

When we are little we are taught to sing "Jesus loves me, this I know, for the Bible tells me so." As we grow older in years and understanding of the teachings of the Bible, we sing "Oh, how I love Jesus, because He first loved me." Yet, it seems that it takes going through something—hard times, the loss of loved ones, or some other difficulty for us to truly realize the truth of the words we sang in our youth and know that "Yes, Jesus loves me."

Having been raised in a family where we were all taught that everyone is made equal, where everyone was considered the same, and where, indeed no one had "special needs," because of his or her mental or physical makeup, it was both difficult and challenging for me when I had a daughter who did have special needs. She was nearly two years old before I realized that she was not progressing at the same rate as other children her age. I watched and waited. When I shared my concern with others, they would say, "Give her time. She's just a baby." I waited some more. Still, things did not fall into place as everyone suggested they would. As far as I could tell, I was losing my child to a world where she seemed encased with no way of getting out for lack of the ability to verbalize her feelings and thoughts.

In spite of her limited ability to communicate, our daughter would often say to her father and me, "Be patient." From where had such simple, yet profound words come? *"Out of the mouth of babes and nursing infants You have perfected praise" (Matthew 21:16).* Hardly from a "baby." Hardly from someone with limited understanding. Yet, she had spoken the words, as clearly and with as much authority as the wisest of the elders. And we tried to do as she had said, to "Be patient." Still, we sought help wherever and whenever possible. We were still losing her, we felt, but we found ways to keep her happy and in good spirits.

Then, time came for her to go to school. Pre-school was great, and the staff at the day care she attended was wonderful in helping and accepting her. We moved, however, by the time she was to begin kindergarten, and that's when the bottom fell out for us. At her new school, our child was treated as if she wasn't welcome, and neither were we. We were told by staff there, "We're doing the best we can for her, but we don't think this is the best place for her. We've never had a child like her here before."

This went on for months, and this was just one of the many battles we had to fight. Somehow we were able to keep her happy, and nothing would make us or allow us to give up. Not even after being told, "She's a nobody and will never be anything," did we give up. That made us fight all the harder. Much of that fight, however, we fought on the knees. Through the many challenges we encountered, I prayed and I prayed, "Lord, give me strength. Lord, show us what to do next." I felt alone, broken, wanted to give up sometimes, wanted to fight harder at other times. And, I prayed, "Lord, have mercy on us . . . on my child."

Then, when the door seemed shut with no way out, when I was just about cried-out, just about doubted-out, when I was not even sure He was listening to my prayers, Jesus stepped in, stood me up, and turned me around. *"It is God who arms me with strength and makes my way perfect" (Psalms 18:32).*

"Where is your faith?" I heard asked from somewhere inside of me. *"And without faith it is impossible to please God" (Hebrews 11:6).* The words came to me over and over like the refrain of a song, while the repeated words of my child, "Be patient" brought joy to my soul. I'd been taught to believe *in* God from an early age, but did I really believe God? Could I really trust that God would be with me in all things, that He would supply *all* my needs, that He would take away the hurt of having, show me how to be a mother to, open doors of opportunity for, and make others accepting of my special needs child? My faith had been untried.

It's easy to believe when the outcome doesn't matter much. It's easy to know that there is a big ol' God of the Universe out there who will supply our daily portion of provisions, but not so easy to believe that He will also take care of the extra-ordinary, as well. How can we know this unless God gives us that situation that in no other way can be resolved but by Him? He gives us such an experience so that we may grasp how wide and long and high and deep is the *love of Christ* for us. It is impossible to come into that very special place with God, that special place of knowing, that special place of feeling His love for us until that faith has been tested and proved.

"God is a rewarder of those who believe and who diligently seek Him" (Hebrews 11:6). Things started to change at the school for the better. There was a turnover in staff, and persons who had controlled things at the school earlier were no longer in place. A new person, with a big heart and a genuine concern for our child's welfare was now in charge. God had *"armed me with strength for battle . . . made my adversaries bow at my feet" (Psalms 18:39).* Joy was restored, and we were able again to smile. Gone were the feelings of guilt and helplessness. Doors were opening not only for our child,

but for many other children, as well. As each door opened, I had only Jesus to thank for it.

I thank Him for the gift of our beautiful daughter, whose own love epitomizes God's love for us—pure, unconditional, and infinite. I thank Him for whispering the words, "Be patient," through her mouth, when I was often ready to give up or about to give out, as a reminder to us to be still and let Him be God. I thank Him for the battles that brought us deeper into the knowledge of Himself and His love. I thank Him for the strength. I thank Him for deliverance. I thank Him for his great love. And now my heart sings, "Oh, how I love Jesus, yes, because I know He loves me so."

But you are a forgiving God,
gracious and compassionate,
slow to anger and abounding in love.
(Nehemiah 9:17)

Sandra Daniel
is a wife and mother of
two natural children and
three step-children.
She enjoys working with children
and is Children's Choir Director,
works with the Children's Dance Ministry,
and is the editor of the Church News.
Sandra is a "Mentor Mom"
with the
Caring House Mentor Moms Program
that mentors young, unwed mothers.
She loves helping people
and truly loves the Lord.

†

$Sandra's$ $Love$ $Story$

I am the only daughter of four children born to my mother and father, so I grew up in a male-dominated household. At the age of 21, I got married and went from my father's house to my husband's house. Whether I wanted to admit it, or even realized it before, the men in my life had always been very important to me. They were the providers. They were the caretakers and the fun makers. They represented security. Therefore, you can not imagine how devastated I was when I became a widow at 39, with two small children who were now depending on me. I had never been responsible, not really, for anyone. My husband of almost 20 years had made all the major decisions in the house, paid all the bills, and did everything from buying the groceries to cooking many of the meals to going to PTA meetings and taking treats to our daughter's classroom for birthday parties and other special occasions. He was the jokester around the house. Though he was often quiet and was known on occasion to drink too much, he was fun, dependable, and an overall nice guy. He was my very best friend.

Then he kissed me on my head one Friday night, said "I'll see ya," and with our 5-year-old son by his side went to sleep for eternity. First thing, I called my daddy to come and help me; then I called the neighbor. My daddy was always the one who could fix it when my husband couldn't, but not this time. My love and my friend since I was 18 years old was forever gone, and, for the first time in my life, I was alone.

When my husband died, I walked around for days, literally, in a fog. I remember there were people around, asking questions, offering their sympathy, and helping out wherever they could, but, it was as if it was all a part of a dream. It wasn't though, and when I woke up, I was faced with a reality that I did not want to face, because it was far too painful.

Though I never blamed God for taking my husband and can't remember ever really questioning Him as to the "why," I could not help feeling let down, let down terribly by God. After all, we were praying people and had tried to "live right," and when you are praying people trying to "live right," everything's supposed to be all right. Nothing bad happens to praying people. Right?

What was I going to do now? My husband was dead, and I had two children to raise. My poor children! How was I going to raise them alone? Our daughter, who was then 15, adored her daddy, and he adored her. He was equally close with our son. "I just can't make it by myself," I cried. At some point in time, I heard the voice of Jesus say in my mind or in my heart, or both, "I will never leave you or forsake you." He assured me that nothing could take place in my life that He and I could not work out together. I heard the voice say, "I know you can bear the loss of your husband, for I am your husband and the father of your children. I will send you an earthly husband in time, and this husband will also be an earthly father to your children." But, I wasn't ready to believe the voice. I was afraid to, I guess—afraid to be let down again.

Amidst the fog, there was incredible pain, then fear and a

deep, deep void. Part of me was gone. After that came the incredible loneliness, followed by shame and self-pity. My husband had
died, while everybody else's was still alive. Something must have
been wrong with me. I didn't want to show my face; so when anyone would come around, I'd excuse myself to the bedroom, close
my door and cry. I decided I couldn't or wouldn't work any longer;
so I stopped. The children and I lived off my husband's social security. I completely withdrew for about eight months.

Behind those closed doors, I hid away not only from
people, but from God, too, I thought. And while there, I decided
that since God had taken my husband, there couldn't possibly be
anything worse that could happen to me. I thought God owed
me something back for what He had taken from me, for the pain
He'd allowed me, after all that praying I'd done. I figured I was
"prayed up," and didn't have to pray anymore. I guess I felt ex-
empt from any further persecution. That line of thinking led me
into a downward spiral leading me farther and farther away from
the Will of God.

I was single again! I joined some longtime, single girlfriends
on a cruise. My husband was not coming back, and it was time to
move on. But instead of my finding my next "Mr. Right" on this
cruise, I met an older man—a minister, at that—who had recently
lost his spouse, as well. He was not even interested in romance; he
just wanted to talk—about scripture and about making it after you
lose your loved one. He did not romance me; he ministered to me.
But I was not interested in being ministered to, and after that first
night talking with him, I hoped not to run into him again because
I didn't want to talk about God anymore. I saw him again the next
day. He kept saying to me, "Don't worry about a man. You can get
along without a man." I didn't know about that, and what about
the promise God had made me about giving me another husband?

Well, I didn't meet my next husband on the cruise, but about
four weeks after the cruise I met a man who I thought would be.

He was younger by ten years. At forty-something, the mother of two, and having been off the dating scene for more than half of my years, I was flattered by the attention of this younger man. I thought, "I got it going on." But from the very start, he was all wrong for me, and the road he took me down was just short of stopping at hell's gate. I was vulnerable and lonely and needed to be loved, and he took full advantage of that. I moved farther and farther away from God. Then, I allowed him to move in with me. It started with the phone calls and a few house parties. I wasn't working, so he would take time off work and we'd spend days together. After he lost his job because of taking too much time off, we'd spend days and nights together. I would send my children to my mother's house. I stopped going to church; somehow I reasoned that I was not worthy to go to church anymore. Even though I started out going after what I thought I wanted, I couldn't get comfortable with the situation. God had let me know early on that this man was not for me, but I told God I could change him. I was going to make him into the man I needed in my life.

When things got so bad, I turned to that God I had withdrawn from, the God I had defied and rebelled against and cried out to Him, "God, please get this man out of my life and out of my house." I couldn't get rid of him. He would leave, but then he would always come back. I cried out to God so much until one day, I heard Him say, "Why have you forsaken me?" Was this His answer to my prayer? Then, he—the man—did the one unforgivable thing, the one thing I would not tolerate; he compromised the well-being of my children. Finally, I had the strength to tell this man to get out. "I'm gonna leave," I said, "and when I get back, I want you gone. I don't want you here anymore."

This relationship robbed me of nearly two years of my life, taking along with it my reputation, my pride, and it almost cost me my relationship with my family. Oddly enough, I had chosen a path of sin because I thought God owed me something for not honoring my prayers and taking my husband. But, the time that He showed me the greatest mercy and evidence of His love did not come after my praying and my trying to live a "good life." It came after I had strayed far from Him. It came when I felt my dirtiest—my lowest—when I felt I deserved it least. "I am your husband . . . I will send you an earthly husband in time," God had said to me. But I did not wait for God. I did not honor Him as my husband and head. I did not trust Him enough, and because of my infidelity, I had suffered greatly. Even then, God rescued me from the hell of an existence I had created for myself. God had looked beyond my faults and saw my needs. I started going to church again. I started praying again.

When I recovered from the nightmare of that relationship, and when I no longer needed or cared if I ever had a man in my life again, God sent to me the husband He had chosen—the husband He had promised. God blessed my life with a husband who, like God Himself, would love me in spite of my sin and former trans-gressions—a husband who would in time teach me what it meant to truly seek God first.

God is a gracious and loving God. He does not repay us according to our sin, but according to His loving kindness. *"Return faithless Israel . . . I will frown on you no longer, for I am merciful . . . I will not be angry forever. Only acknowledge your guilt—you have rebelled against the Lord your God . . . and have not obeyed me . . . Return faithless people . . . for I am your husband . . ."* (Jeremiah 3:12-14). And when you do return to Him, He is there with loving and open arms to receive you, no matter what.

Surely He took up our infirmities
and carried our sorrows . . .
He was pierced for our transgressions,
He was crushed for our iniquities . . .
and by His wounds we are healed.
(Isaiah 53:4-5)

Deborah Raglin Green
was raised by her loving parents,
Rev. and Mrs. M.L. Raglin.
Deborah is a graduate of
Morris Brown College and
a member of
Alpha Kappa Alpha Sorority, Inc.
She is the mother
of two children
and currently
resides in Atlanta, GA.

✝

$Deborah's$ $Love$ $Story$

How do you know that your mother and your father love you? Well, as a child, you might answer, because they give you stuff. You might even say that they love you because they're there for you. Or you might think of all the make-you-feel-good things they do and say. Yes, that's how you may know they love you. On the other hand, you probably would not identify their love for you by the gifts they didn't give, the things they didn't do, the times they said, "No," or the occasions when they did not appear to be there for you. That's just not the way to see or realize somebody's love for you. But, sometimes that's exactly where the answer lies. You may not get such an understanding of parents, however, until much later in life, if at all, and even then such understanding is a gift.

For the first six weeks of my life, my parents were faced with the decision of whether or not to give me up for adoption. When the decision was made, they decided to give me to my paternal grandparents, who accepted me with welcoming arms. *"Though my father and mother forsake me, the LORD will receive me"* (Psalms

27:10). I believe that was the beginning of Jesus' love being shown toward me. My grandfather was a Baptist minister and a good one at that, so being brought up in a Christian home, I had always heard about God and Jesus. At the early age of five or six, I accepted the Lord Jesus into my life and joined my grandfather's church. I believed in God and Jesus, but to what extent did I believe? I don't know. When I was six years old, my grandparents adopted me and became my legal parents. That was Jesus' love shown to me again. There were so many other paths my life could have taken. My biological mother could have made different choices, like leaving me in a trash can or leaving me on someone's door step, or worse than that, she could have aborted me. Instead, she chose to give me to someone she knew would love me and take care of me.

Although I had always been told the truth about my beginning, as I grew older, I began to wonder about my biological parents, "Why didn't they want me? Was I not good enough for them or what?" Well, you know time does have its way of revealing things to us. I began to get answers when I was 34 years old. It all started when I was asked to attend a family reunion for my birth mother's family. When I showed some signs of hesitation, my adopted father sat down with me and answered many of my questions. Not only was I relieved to get those answers, but I also began to get the validation I so needed. Again, Jesus was showing His love to me. When my father insisted that I go because these were my "blood relatives" and because I needed to "know my roots," I went. There I received more answers, more validation, and the start of a beautiful relationship with a family I had never known. More of Jesus' love.

But, knowing that Jesus loved me up to this point was like the equivalent of the child who knows of the parents' love because of the stuff they give or because they were "there" for you. I would not come to know the extent of God's love for me, that kind of love that is realized through pain or through those "it's-gonna-hurt-me-more-than-it-hurts-you" experiences that you have with your parents, until some years later when I moved to Plymouth, Minnesota with my son and daughter. This is the place where God paid me a personal visit; this is where He made good on His promise to comfort me, *"As a mother comforts her child, so will I comfort you"* (Isaiah 66:13), where He took care of me, and finally where He restored life to my body. It was not at church; it was at my home on my couch. God can visit you in all kind of places, you know, and His timing is always perfect. Sometimes God has to separate us from familiar surroundings and from our loved ones so that He can get our attention. He wants us to get closer to Him, so that He can get closer to us.

In December of the year after I made that huge move to Minnesota from my home in Atlanta, I developed what I thought was a skin rash on my arms. I went to the doctor. Medical treatment for inflamed hair follicles proved futile. Two days later the rash had moved over 50 percent of my body. Additional treatment with an antihistamine resulted in an allergic reaction. A biopsy was performed, and I was diagnosed with psoriasis. By this time the psoriasis had covered over 95 percent of my body. Being in this place that was so far away from everything and everybody that I knew, and being stricken with this disease, really sent me overboard.

I was alone and indeed at the mercy of my doctor and God. Although I could not comprehend it through my pain, Jesus was working all along and showing His love for me! The dermatologist who God sent me to or who God sent to me had never treated an African American for psoriasis before, but agreed to treat me. When all else failed, he recommended chemotherapy. He felt that if chemotherapy worked on Caucasians, it should work on me, but emphasized that he did not know what the chemo would do to me, or even if it would work. I took chemotherapy every Friday and then slept through the entire weekend. Treatment lasted for 16 weeks, during which time my skin shed—my complete outer skin including the skin on my hands and feet. My fingernails even separated from the skin. I lost my hair, and every night around nine o'clock, I had uncontrollable itching. During this time, I noticed that when I changed clothes I would hear something like small grains of sand hitting the floor. I gave little or no thought to this until I began to clean the tile floors in the bathroom. It was then I discovered that the small grains of sand that were hitting the floor were my skin shedding. It was during this time I discovered the true meaning of the phrase *"dust thou art, and unto dust shalt thou return" (Genesis 3:19)*.

I don't remember, but my friends said that when they'd call me and ask how I was doing, I would reply, "As long as God is with me, I will be okay." I remember praying and telling God that if He would stay by my side, I knew that I would be all right. I really felt God's love for me in the healing from the psoriasis. I felt a calmness that I had never felt before. I felt good from the inside out to just see the miracle of my body being transformed right in front of my eyes.

I wish I had taken pictures. I looked horrible. Losing my hair and shedding my skin were the worst things that I had ever experienced; however, this experience allowed me to see God's goodness working in my life. It proved to me that God cared about me and that He cared enough about me to peel away the old, the dirty, the painful and undesirable parts of me and cover me with a brand new layer of His beauty and righteousness.

I was that pot spoken of in Jeremiah which the potter found *"marred in his hands; so the potter formed it into another pot, shaping it as it seemed best to him" (Jeremiah 18:4)*. No matter what I may have done in the past, He had forgiven me, and He healed my body to demonstrate His love and forgiveness. There is a line from a song that says, "If you wanna see a miracle, just look at me."* I say look at me and you will see not only a miracle but also living proof of God's love and healing power. To Him be the glory!

---

*   Chicago Mass Choir, "I'm Blessed," *Calling on You: Live,* New Haven Records, March 6, 2001.

Yes, Jesus Loves Me

Surely it was for my benefit
that I suffered such anguish.
In Your love You kept me
from the pit of destruction;
You have put all my sins
behind Your back.
(Isaiah 38:17)

Mary Wingate
is married and has two sons,
Jacob and Lucas.
Mary is a Registered Nurse
and currently works as a
Job Developer,
representing individuals
with disabilities.
She and her family
live in Beaumont, TX.

✝

Mary W's Love Story

Growing up in Orange, Texas (last stop in Texas before hitting Louisiana and the Gulf of Mexico), I was the ninth child of eighteen children—nine boys and nine girls—yes, all from the same mother and father. Anyway, as good Catholic families did, we attended a Catholic school, at that time still run by nuns.

Life always seemed chaotic—which was the norm for a family this size. Looking back, I believe the chaos came more from living in an alcoholic family, than from the size of the family, though at the time I did not realize my father was alcoholic. He just drank a lot of beer. My mother instilled in us sound morals—emphasizing a type of secular virtue system. Daddy made us say the rosary every night—on our knees—as soon as the TV show, "Gunsmoke," was over.

Like all siblings, we fought and played a lot. We knew God was always there and "watching." If we lied, said a curse word under our breath, thought bad thoughts, or missed a single Sunday Mass (our moral obligation), we knew we had better hit the first confession we could attend, to confess the sin. Otherwise, we would go straight to hell or at least burn away in purgatory for a miserable length of time. You see, God was a just God, and She kept score. We *knew* this, so we had no one to blame but ourselves when we screwed up. The Sisters at school reminded us of this often.

After high school for me, there was college. I graduated with a nursing degree, worked a while as an RN and then returned to college for another degree. Before finishing my second degree, I did another traditional thing, I married a fellow—Catholic, of course. When I'd finished this degree, I went back for a master's degree. My husband had decided to return to college, and I reasoned, "Why shouldn't I?" Having no children and being the driven person I was, and looking for ways to fill my time, I became extremely active in sports. I qualified for an area state women's competitive soccer team and played when not working in the emergency room or studying.

Being the strong-willed person that I am, and being filled with a competitive sense of fair play, I became very active in different civic and community activities in an effort to improve what I considered to be "bad situations." Meanwhile, my marriage suffered, and so did my spiritual life. I tried hard to find God as a loving God but seemed to not quite connect. I became very distrustful of the Catholic Church because of its poor treatment of women (by men, of all people!).

I started attending a local Presbyterian church where men and women seemed to be able to participate in the family of God as God Herself had intended. This did not fill the hole in my heart, however. During this time, my husband and I started a family and ended up with two fine sons—born 12 months apart. After the birth of our second son, I became horribly depressed. My marriage soon deteriorated to the point of my husband becoming physically and verbally abusive. I fell into a deep state of hopelessness, with no sense of self-worth. Literally, I was unable to function.

Before long, I started writing prescriptions for myself (remember, I was an RN) in an attempt to clear the fogginess out of my head. I was in such a state that I knew I was unable to hold down a job, but at the same time I was desperate to do so. How else could I divorce my husband and support two young sons and myself? The prescription writing increased as my ability to function decreased. I felt as if I were literally losing my mind. I cried for hours at a time. I was afraid to leave my marriage. At the same time, I feared that by staying in this hostile environment I would train my sons, by example, how to be depressed, angry and abusive men and husbands. As much as I wanted to, I did not know how to leave.

Finally, I was arrested when my youngest son was 1½ years old, while attempting to fill a fraudulent prescription. After that, my husband and I did divorce, but my problems continued and soon escalated—especially after my husband obtained physical sole custody of my babies. I was arrested again, and this time I was sent to prison—for lying, of all things. The judge knew I was guilty and was prepared to let me go if I would admit my problem, but I refused to admit it. Whether because of pride or for some other unexplainable reason, I remained in denial. After all, look at everything else I accomplished in my life *on my own* before all this trouble started. Surely, I would find a way out of this.

But I did not. Instead I received a five-year prison sentence. I lost my children, my jobs, respect—that of self and of others, my nursing license, and all remaining hope. I was heavily in debt, and my credit took a nose dive. I was so, so ashamed. Now, everyone knew the truth! I was ridden with guilt. Look at all the pain and suffering I had caused innocent people. People had tried to help me, but I remained in denial and refused their help. After all, I was self-reliant, and I would change things if I simply worked hard enough and would not give up. Well, it was time to give up.

All my self-reliance and determination and self-will were

shattered. My husband was suing for sole custody and to end my parental rights. What could I do to stop all this from happening from inside a women's prison? Sitting on my top prison bunk (C3-9), I cried my heart out. I would not see my sons start school. I would not see them again until they were 11 and 12 years of age! What agony and shame I felt!

Then the miracle occurred. In the midst of my crying, I suddenly stopped and started praying. I saw myself as a little child with my head buried in the Virgin Mary's arms, crying. Mary was consoling me, telling me that as a mother, she had also felt the torment and heartbreak of losing a son. At that point, I knew that God loved me, no matter what, because I was a child of God! Could the Virgin Mary or I ever quit loving one of our children because they did something *bad?* Of course not! We would just want them to realize what they had done, repent and change their ways so that they could again *feel* their parent's love, which had always been there from the beginning. Was God not my supreme parent? If I could not stop loving my children, then how could God stop loving me? God could not and would not. GOD LOVED ME NO MATTER WHAT!

Another miracle: my total length of stay in prison was four months, not five years as set! My family stood by me—they, too, loved me. Different family members, friends and other loved ones kept me forever in their prayers. Like God could not—they did not forget me! Now, after being reunited with my sons for over three years, my sons have been so forgiving. My youngest son told me, "Mama, just because you went to jail does not mean you're a bad person. Jesus was put in jail, and He is God!" This young son of mine healed me more than anyone else could, simply by letting God's love shine through him—and touching me!

Since that time, I have grown to understand the depth of a father's love for his son in the parable, *"The Prodigal Son,"* as well as from the message in a verse from Isaiah, *"Can a mother forget the*

Yes, Jesus Loves Me

baby at her breast and have no compassion on the child she has borne? Though she may forget, I will not forget you" (Isaiah 49:15). I am not forgotten.

Praise the Lord . . .
who forgives all your sins
and heals all your diseases,
who redeems your life from the pit
and crowns you with love and compassion,
who satisfies your desires with good things . . .
He does not treat us as our sins deserve
or repay us according to our iniquities.
For as high as the heavens are above the earth,
so great is His love for those who fear Him;
as far as the east is from the west,
so far has He removed our transgressions from us.
(Psalms 103:2-5,10-12)

Gladys Carlin
was born and raised in
Fargo, ND. Gladys became involved
in a 12-step recovery program
in 1976 when she was
17 years old and at that time
really began to search for
a personal relationship with God.
She moved to Texas
when she was 19 years old
and has been sober since June of 1978.
"The experience I had when
Jesus became so real to me," Gladys says,
"has been only the beginning
of a wonderful relationship
with God."
She remarried in May of 1989,
and she and her husband
have been blessed with three children.

✝

$Gladys'$ $Love$ $Story$

"The Sign"

I was raised in a church-going household. When I was growing up, my parents carried me to church every Sunday, where I was
in the choir and involved in the youth organization. But in spite of
this exposure, God loomed large and distant and far out of my
reach. Although I grew up with a supportive family, it was not a
home where affection was openly or often expressed. My perception about my relationship to God often mirrored my perception
about my relationship to my family and the world. I felt so small
and unimportant that I did not feel God could really care about
me. As I grew older, so did these feelings grow. Everywhere I went,
I felt like I did not belong. I felt so empty inside, and I longed to be
filled. Just short of my sixteenth birthday, I took my first drink of
alcohol and did not stop drinking until I got very drunk. The alcohol numbed my feelings of isolation, of unworthiness, of emptiness, and of being unloved. Suddenly, I didn't care what other people

thought of me. I didn't feel out of place anymore. I had found that something to fill the emptiness. Alcohol, I thought, was better than God could ever be!

But, the feeling was short-lived. In fact, I never got that same feeling from drinking again, although I continued to try for the next year and a half. By the time I turned seventeen, I had a drinking problem that was threatening to consume me or kill me—either of which meant certain destruction. Then, by what I now know to be the grace of God, two teen-aged alcoholics came one day to talk to my high school sociology class. As these two girls told their stories, I felt they were telling mine—their feelings, their experiences were so familiar to me. When they were finished, I knew where I could go for help, and I did. The group these girls unknowingly invited me to become a part of not only helped to save my life, but they also reintroduced me to, or perhaps introduced me to, really, for the first time, the God who before was too big for me, the God I felt could not possibly love me, the God I had strayed from. Because of their efforts and the love they showed me, I began to slowly open up to the possibility that this God thing was okay. Even so, I did not yet feel Him in my heart.

To satisfy that longing, I went looking elsewhere. I felt like I had to be around people to feel loved, and I found a guy who gave me a lot of attention. When I was 19 years old, we started living together and soon married, against my parents' warnings. Even his parents told me they felt we were making a mistake. I would not listen. We ended up in Texas, about 1200 miles from home and family. I stayed sober for a while, but whether out of boredom or my extreme unhappiness with my new husband, I was lured back onto that treacherous road to the "good life." My husband and I started smoking dope together, which led to much other immoral activity. Both of us had sexual relationships outside of our marriage—many of them. My husband even wanted me to prostitute for him so that he could support his drug habit. I was too afraid to do it, and I thank God for that! I was more miserable than I had ever been. I was afraid I would die, either at someone else's hands or my own. I could not continue living the way I was.

An older couple that had befriended me helped me to escape from my situation. In a very old model car, with all I owned crammed into it and ten dollars I had borrowed from the lawyer who was helping me get my divorce, I set out from Bay City, Texas to Houston to enter a halfway house. Feeling very scared and very alone, I still was not sure I was doing the right thing. I considered stopping to buy a bottle of alcohol, but knew that I didn't have enough money to reach oblivion. As I got nearer to Houston, doubts crowded my mind. I wondered why I just didn't call my parents, who lived up north, and ask them to send me some money to come home. I felt like such a failure. I seriously contemplated driving off the side of the freeway into oncoming traffic, but didn't want to kill anyone but myself. As I was looking around for the best place to end it all, I saw a small, hand-made sign by the side of the road. It simply said, "JESUS LOVES YOU."

A shiver traveled up my spine. I pulled over to the side of the road, and began to cry. Could Jesus really love ME? After all I had done, was that possible? I started to remember some of the things I was taught in my younger years in church about the life and teachings of Jesus— *"For God so loved the world that He gave His only Son to die, so that those who believe will have eternal life"* (John 3:16). *"Blessed are those who hunger and thirst for righteousness, for they will be filled"* (Matthew 5:6). So many things which I had been taught as I grew up began to come back to me, and they began to make some sense. As I wept there, I felt as if Jesus was putting his arms around me and holding me close to comfort me. I knew with certainty in my heart that I was doing God's will by going to Houston to enter the halfway house and begin my life anew. I knew this because He had given me "a sign" that called out His love to me from the side of the road. It was a sign that persuaded me for the first time that Jesus had suffered for me on that cross and that I never had to go through anything alone again. I don't know how long I sat there, crying and feeling the love of Jesus for me. But I do know that when I wiped away my tears, I felt as if my soul was washed clean. I started up my car, carefully merged with traffic, and headed to Houston. But this time, I knew I was not alone.

God has poured out His love into our hearts
by the Holy Spirit, whom He has given us.
You see, at just the right time,
when we were still powerless,
Christ died for the ungodly . . .
God demonstrates His own love for us in this:
While we were still sinners, Christ died for us.
(Romans 5:5-8)

Brenda Banks
lives in the
Houston, Texas area.
and is married to Tommy.
They have one c
ollege-aged son.
Brenda enjoys bunco, tennis and golf.
She also enjoys travel
and has made trips to
Russia, China,
Finland, and Mexico
on joint
international missions.

✝

Day 20

Brenda's Love Story

"When God Became Real"

"For whoever wants to save his life will lose it,
but whoever loses his life for me will find it" (Matthew 16:25).

God set me up for a fall—God and my grandmother's prayers, I might add. My grandfather dealt in the occult. He was my father's father, and the "tonics" he sold were sought after by folks from miles and miles around. My grandmother prayed. She was my mother's mother, and she was a praying, believing, and God-fearing woman. These things, along with the rugged individualism of my father's side and the loving and kindheartedness of my mother's side, account for the dichotomy that existed in my family overall, and within me personally. My father imparted to me the value of the dollar, i.e., materialism, while my mother sought to impart to me her faith and caring for others.

At various times and in various numbers, my grandmother,

Yes, Jesus Loves Me

121

who didn't live very far from us when we were growing up, would have all 13 of her daughter's children come to her home, where we had to kneel before her as she prayed mighty prayers for us—for our salvation, and our protection. She would also have us sit on the "Mourner's Bench" in the little church in the small-town community in Louisiana where I grew up, and there we'd receive the prayers of the church for our salvation and deliverance. Then one night during a revival meeting at the church, when the preacher extended the invitation, "If you want to be saved, come on up," I went. In an effort to appease the preacher and my grandmother, I went. My brother, who was sleeping on my shoulder and fell over when I got up, went too. If I had thought that would stop my grandmother's prayers or lessen them, I was mistaken, because after that she prayed more fervently, and in addition to her prayers, insisted upon us praying our own prayers every time we went over to her house.

But as an adult, I had put all of that behind me, and life was going just fine. I was a rising star. As I blew out the candles on my 26th birthday cake, I was feeling pretty special. I had it all, or, at the very least, the hope of having it all. I was young, well-educated, well-employed, married, and had recently given birth to the one of the one-point-five children that at that time made up the "ideal" American family. My star shone brightly on that day as my co-workers at the major oil company where I worked unveiled a surprise celebration for me. Soon after this celebration, however, I and the guys and gals who had become my closest and dearest friends would be shipping off to various places around the country to begin building careers and lives. My star would set over Houston, Texas. When I arrived for my new assignment at the Houston Terminal, where the marketing crew had its offices, I found a group of very independent, mostly private, and highly competitive sales associates. The unspoken rule at the Houston Terminal was that there had never been a successful Black female sales representative. I silently vowed to become the first.

At first, the territory was pretty easy to manage. Then, I began to notice that when I made sales calls to my local stations, the managers did not give me the same respect and treatment as I'd observed them giving to the "Reps" that trained me in the territory. I responded to this by becoming somewhat of a tyrant. I bossed the station managers around. They complained, and the powers-that-be responded by reassigning me to the Finance Department.

The generous perks I had become accustomed to were all but gone in my new assignment in the Finance Department. Management assured me that my stay would be temporary and that I was just to learn the overall operations, not do the job. But, I did end up doing the job, and not very well, I might add. Never in all of my MBA training and high goal setting did I imagine I would actually have to do such menial work. I had a huge chip on my shoulder and was ashamed to tell people what I actually did. Though I did not know it, I was being set up. God was beginning to work on the very root of my problem: *pride,* and my grandmother's prayers were being answered. But, it certainly did not occur to me that my struggles in the workplace had anything to do with those prayers, or that God was trying to get my attention and was using these harsh circumstances to do it. I had simply made my bed, and now I had to lie in it.

My ambition had suffered a terrible blow; my ego was severely wounded, and my faith, hardly discernible, was not even a factor to be considered. My life was difficult. I found little joy in my work, but I found much joy in raising my son. In fact, I poured a lot of my energy into raising and teaching him. I spared no expense on various little educational toys and games to give him a good start. Some relief came when I met Kris at work. She was friendly, easygoing, well-liked and respected by her peers, as well as by management. Kris invited me to lunch, showed me around, introduced me to others, and made me feel accepted. I am convinced that God sent Kris to be an angel on earth to me. Then, one day she invited me to attend a noon Bible Study with her and a few other ladies from the office. I joined them. Kris had such a disarming way about her, such a sincerity and genuineness. You could feel her love; you could almost feel God's love through her. There's a song that says, "They'll know we are Christians by our love, by our love."* That's the way it was with Kris.

About the same time that Kris was showing me Jesus in her attitude and actions, I met Pat. Pat, from my neighborhood, had been inviting me to something called a "cell" group meeting. After attending Bible Study with Kris, I finally had the courage to attend one of those meetings, but felt quite uncomfortable at first. Each time I entered Pat's home I felt a terrible weight on my shoulders. It was as if I carried a sack of bricks on my back. I didn't like that feeling.

In spite of the terrible weight I felt when I went to those meetings, I felt compelled to continue going. Then, one night, Pat and her husband asked if there was anybody who wanted to receive Jesus. It was almost the same question I'd heard and responded to during that revival meeting when I was a child at my grandmother's church, but this time my response had nothing to do with pleasing the preacher or my grandmother. Jesus said, *"Come to me, all you who are weary and burdened, and I will give you rest" (Matthew 11:28).* After a few songs, I went up to the fireplace and with Pat standing beside me, holding my hand and guiding me in prayer, I accepted His love. Though I did not realize it immediately, the weight was lifted from my back. I know now that it had been the weight of sin.

Though I had hitched my star, my hope of rising high and far, to the material; though I operated behind a cloud of insecurity and skepticism, God's love found me—sent me angels— and removed the weight that would ultimately destroy me. In the midst of my personal struggle between good and evil, between worldliness and godliness, God had reached down with His loving hand and lifted me out. His *love* had lifted me, and not just for my own sake, but for the sake of those other family members who still walked in darkness. Yes, I know that Jesus loves me, and I walk in that love daily.

My challenges as a Christian, wife, mother, employee, you name it, continue until this very day; but I am always sure of His Love and protection for me. Through the many challenges God has delivered me, He has given me what I now call my life verse, *"I know the plans I have for you . . . Plans to prosper you and not to harm you, plans to give you hope and a future"* (Jeremiah 29:11). He has indeed given me a future and a hope.

---

*   *They'll Know We are Christians by Our Love,* Words and music by Peter Scholtes, ©1967 by F.E.L. Publications, Ltd., Las Vegas, Nevada.

Let not your heart be troubled;
you believe in God, believe also in Me.
In My Father's house are many mansions;
if it were not so, I would have told you.
I go to prepare a place for you.
And if I go and prepare a place for you,
I will come again and receive you to Myself;
that where I am, there you may be also.
(John 14:1-3 — NKJV)

Rosemary Rice-Jones
has worked as
an educator for
25 years
serving in the capacity of teacher,
elementary counselor,
assistant principal and principal.
She is a wife, mother of one
and stepmother of three.

✝

Day 21

Rosemary's Love Story

My mother has taught me some of the greatest and most memorable lessons of my life. And, although she could not, nor could any other human being, bring me into the personal knowledge of God's love for me, she was very much a part of the experience that led me into such knowledge. Surprisingly, or maybe not, many things are born of pain—many great and wonderful things that we would perhaps otherwise miss because of our desire to avoid painful experiences. Such was the case with my mother. Out of her pain—out of our mutual pain—was born the great revelation of God's love.

She screamed; she yelled; she cried out. She cried out to God, "Please take me." She wanted relief—relief from the pain and agony of her illness. I stood by her side, helpless. What could I do? I could do nothing but hold her hand, rub it, and tell her she would be okay. She cried. I cried. My mother was writhing in pain. She was asking God to please take her home with Him. She cried. Pleaded. Prayed.

I was praying also that God would hear her prayer and answer her prayer. Was I praying for my mother to die? No, I was praying for my mother to be at peace. I wanted her to be comfortable. God, what I really wanted was for MY mother to return to me; I didn't even know the woman I saw lying in the bed before me. She prayed. I got angry.

All my life, it had been drilled into my being that God cares for us. This assurance had guided me and given me comfort in good times and bad. I had been a proud recipient of God's love. But, it was the dating-stage kinda love that I had worn so proudly, not the marriage-stage love that is revealed after years of togetherness in all kinda weather. It was love that had not yet been tried—had not yet been proven.

I continued to ask myself why bad things were happening to this good and kind person, who was my mother. No answers were forthcoming, even as I would regroup and pray more fervently in my own daily prayers. My mother had become a mere shadow of the woman I had once known and loved. But, I still loved her! Why else would the pain have been so great—right? It was most difficult for me that she seemed to know who I was on fewer and fewer occasions when I would travel the 700 miles to visit her.

I became so low and full of woe that I could no longer pray. I was simply all prayed out. I had prayed to God that He grant my mother peace and comfort. Why wasn't He listening to me? I questioned Him further, "God, where is that compassion that fails not? Can't you see that my mother needs Your help? She is old; she is in pain. She has lived a good life. God, why are you punishing us? She is in physical pain, and I am in mental pain."

Answers from God come in strange and unexpected ways. I felt so angry—so abandoned by God that I could not easily discern His answers, but when the meaning came, it was both startling and simple. That is often how God speaks to us.

It was not until after my mother returned to the nursing

home after a five-day hospital stay that I came to understand why God had not "answered" my mother's prayers—or mine. Ms. Ollie, my mother's roommate until the time she left for the hospital, had really been worried about my mother; so I went to tell her Mom was back, but in another unit of the nursing home. Ms. Ollie could, no doubt, see how distressed I was. In her quiet and determined manner, she said to me, "Honey, her mansion is not ready yet." I heard her speak, but did not respond. For a minute, I thought Ms. Ollie was not lucid. But she continued, "God won't be ready for her until He finishes her mansion. He is not going to call her home until He is ready for her." *"Let not your heart be troubled . . . In my Father's house are many mansions . . . I go to prepare a place for you"* *(John 14:1-2).*

I just stood there with tears streaming down my cheeks. Ms. Ollie's remark offered a quiet, but assured reminder to me that it is God who takes care of the business of preparing mansions and handing out robes and crowns. It is His business to call His loved ones home in His appointed time. It was a quiet, but powerful reminder that God is in control. Always.

I found rest in the thought that my mother will only leave this earth when God is ready for her—when He has completed that place that He went to especially prepare for her. And somewhere in the reverberation of Ms. Ollie's words, I could hear, "Be still and know . . ." that while you are fretting, I am working things out for your good. That while you are angry with me and cannot understand my ways, while you even doubt me, I love you still—with an everlasting love. That while you are feeling lonely and abandoned by your loved ones and feeling abandoned by Me, as well, I am right here with you as I said I'd always be. Be still. And know. I am YOUR God.

Dear friends, let us love one another,
for love comes from God . . .

God is love.

This is how God showed His love among us:
He sent His one and only Son into the world
that we might live through Him.
This is love: not that we loved God,
but that He loved us
and sent His Son as an atoning sacrifice for our sins.

Dear friends, since God so loved us,
we also ought to love one another . . .
if we love one another, God lives in us
and His love is made complete in us.
(1 John 4:7-12)

Lorraine Mason
immigrated to the United States
over 20 years ago after a military coup
in her beloved country, Liberia,
forced many people to flee and
seek refuge in various countries around the world.
She settled in Houston, Texas
where she completed her
undergraduate degree at the
University of Houston. Today,
she is a Licensed Grief Psychotherapist
and a member of the
Association of Oncology Social Work
(AOSW) and the
North American Christian Social Worker
(NACSW). She is married to Fulkra
and is the mother of three wonderful children,
Varnie, Janjay and Justinian.
She recently relocated and
now resides in Harrisburg, PA.

✝

Lorraine's Love Story

"How many times must I prove how much I love you,
How many ways must my love for you I show,
How many times must I rescue you from trouble,
For you to know just how much I love you?"*
—The Brooklyn Tabernacle Choir

These words are a constant reminder to me of God's continuous presence in my life. As well, they are a reminder of the many times I have taken His presence for granted or did not attribute events in my life to His Divine intervention. But this love of God that I now know, was not the kind of love I learned about early in my life. I would not come to know this love until much later.

As a child, growing up in Liberia, West Africa, I lived in the midst of a family of women who knew and loved the Lord. That meant always going to church and being a decent human being to all of God's creatures: mankind and creatures of other kinds, both great and small. I remember my Grandma Mary Jane and her sister,

Grandaunt Lucinda, instilling the fear of God in us about how important it was to love and care for all beings, even for animals. We were taught that if animals were treated badly by my siblings or me, on the Day of Judgment, we would have to be accountable to God, even for them. So, when we would see a poor worm struggling to get out of the sun, it would not be unusual for one of us to kind of "help it along" to safety. They taught us "love" very early on.

But in teaching us to love others and all things, they also taught us that God's love was punitive and full of wrath. His love was a thing with dire consequences. As a child at such an early age, it was chilling to think that Our Father, who sent His Son to die for us, could also subject us to hell and damnation. At the age of seven, I left the town of Marshall where my grandmother and her sister lived for a much larger metropolitan city, where I, for the first time, attended an all-girls Catholic school. What I learned there was much different from what those beloved older women in my life had taught me. In the Catholic school I attended, they did not teach hell and damnation or God's wrath, at least not the same brand of it as my elders taught. Instead, I was introduced to a religion of intervention to the Father by a priest through confession, to a religion of reciting rosaries and petitioning the saints to intercede on our behalf for sins untold, while at the same time fearing God for what He could do to those who broke His commandments.

Then there were the missionaries who also helped to shape my spiritual and religious beliefs. They often preached about the roads of good and evil and suffering. Later on in my life, I would read *Sinners in the Hands of an Angry God,* which reinforced all those negative attributes I had been taught in my earlier years, none of which were balanced with the teaching that "God is love." It was no wonder that I decided early on in my life that it was better to do and be good than to experience the wrath of God and burn in eternal hell.

As I grew older, no matter how much I saw God work in

my mother's life or in other people's lives, I did not embrace Him as an all-loving God. I did not embrace Him for all the unseen things He had guided me through. I did not embrace Him when He brought me unharmed through the coup that killed many in my country in 1980. I did not embrace Him when He allowed me to give birth, almost painlessly to my son, at an age when some thought I was too young to do so. Neither did I embrace Him when He gave me the wisdom and resources to raise this child, despite my age and the fact that I was so far away from home. I did not embrace him when He blessed me with a loving husband, a man who sought to know the depths of my heart and to build a life and home with me based on our shared values. I did not embrace Him even when I realized He was always giving me another chance at life to get it right. Nor did I embrace Him when He put a shield of protection over my seven brothers and sisters and other relatives who were caught in the midst of war. Not even entirely in the moment of my mother's death did I embrace Him. Little did I know, however, that it would be the death of this woman whom I loved more than any other in life that would be the catalyst for my coming to realize and to truly embrace God's love.

It was a Sunday evening. My husband was out of the city, and my young three-year-old daughter accompanied me to church. I had recently started attending this church where, by this time, my soul was being fed and my spirit lifted. I had joined the choir and had begun to feel like I really belonged. However, on this particular evening all I wanted to do was sing and go home. I tried to make a discreet exit and go pick up my daughter who was attending the children's service. She, however, put up such a protest that being discreet was not possible. Embarrassed to have anyone know I was "skipping out" on church, and in an effort to draw no further attention, I decided to make my way back to the sanctuary and take in the service. A blessing awaited me that I could not have imagined.

A lot had happened to me since my mother's death. I'd given

birth to two children, children I'm sure that she had prayed for. My emotions had run the gamut, ranging from anger to hurt to abandonment. Then there were times I just felt a tremendous void had enveloped my life—a void that I just couldn't seem to get rid of—a void that I felt God had created by taking away my mother. Such void had made it impossible for me to revel in the long awaited births of my son and daughter. Instead, I battled feelings of depression and rejection. I longed for conversations with my mother. I looked for her, but could not find her. I sought her in numerous futile relationships that I pursued to compensate for the one I had lost. All the while, I never gave God a second thought. After all, I wasn't looking to be chastised. I was looking to be accepted—unconditionally. I was looking to be loved. I was a decent person. Didn't most people in my life like me? Didn't they like who I was and what I stood for? Didn't they? Then, why the void? Why the emptiness?

The Praise Team began to sing. Never before had I been so aware as I was at that very moment of how much I hungered and thirsted for God's love and reassurance. *"All to Jesus I surrender, All to Him I freely give,"* they sang. Somewhere in the midst of the singing in that church on that night, an awareness of the hunger and thirst flooded my thoughts. I longed to be in communion with God. I had so much to talk with Him about. I had had conversations with Him before, but it seemed I was always the one doing the talking and never the listening. I had never stood still long enough to listen, to get feedback, to hear Him out. This time would be different. I would worship, praise and adore Him. I would be reverent in His presence. I would give Him charge over me completely. This time I would listen. *"I will ever love and trust Him, In His presence daily live."* I listened, and I heard Him. I heard Him speak to me as I had never heard Him speak before, "Why do you look to others to validate you?" *"All to Jesus I surrender, Lord I give myself to Thee."*

Yes, Jesus Loves Me

Then, I heard Him say, "Pray for the spirit of your mother." As He spoke to me, I remained focused and connected. "Don't you know how much I love you?" I heard Him ask. Then, He seemed to ask me what it would take for me to realize this. At that time, I knew I had to embrace what He was offering me with all of my being. *"Fill me with Thy love and power, Let Thy blessing fall on me."* In my heart I responded, "Yes, Lord, I do," but I didn't want to just say it. I wanted to believe it, embrace it, and claim it as my own. And, I did! *"I surrender all, I surrender all; All to Thee, my blessed Saviour, I surrender all."***

Since then, He has shown me every day and in every way how His love and tender mercies have carried me and continue to carry me through many a times. And today, I not only embrace that love, but rejoice in it with all my heart, with all my soul and with every fiber of my being.

*   Carol Cymbala, *So You Would Know,* High and Lifted Up, Atlantic Recording Corp., 1999.

**   *I Surrender All,* Words by Jueson W. Van Deventer, 1896.

Though the mountains be shaken
and the hills be removed,
yet my unfailing love for You will not be shaken.
(Isaiah 54:10)

Ruth Ollison
is Senior Pastor of
Beulah Land Community Church
in Houston's Third Ward area.
Her ministry began in earnest
after a radio and television
broadcasting career that
spanned over two decades.
Her passion is making disciples
for Jesus Christ
and teaching others to do the same.
She is the wife of Quincy
and the mother of Jacob.

†

Ruth's Love Story

I do not deserve to be perceived as any kind of example of a relationship with the Lord. Though Jesus has saved me, and has sought me, and revealed many mysteries to me, and has blessed me beyond measure, I still find myself being unfaithful to Him. It is a disappointing, but true admission after all these years.

I would like to be writing this treatise from a position of total intimacy, but instead I am writing from a state of total disappointment in myself. Because of compromise. More and more, I am discovering that the things that get in the way of the best things in life are the good things, not the bad things I used to do. A case in point occurred last Friday. I have a standing date with the Lord each Friday. It is His day. Well, of course, each day is His day, but in my life, Friday has become the day that I devote myself totally to Him. Whatever the Lord wants to do, we do; wherever the Lord wants to go, we go. I am open to hearing whatever the Lord wants to say to me.

This past Friday, I thought it not robbery to spend the time with our son. He was out of school for the day, and it had been a while since we were able to hang out together; so I reasoned within myself that Jake and I would have Friday, and the Lord and I would have Sunday. This was done without prayer, without checking with the Lord at all. I just knew the Lord would understand. After all, He wants me to be a good mother, and . . . (you can fill in the rest with any of a number of good excuses). Well, it did not stop there on this Friday. There was a call from one of the members of the church who had a friend whom he had not seen for eight years coming into the large airport. The church member asked where the airport was. I sensed immediately that what he really wanted was a ride to the airport and for me to take him to find his friend. Again, I reasoned. Truly with the volume of traffic, the maze of terminals, and increased security measures, the airport can be a daunting place for someone who does not fly often. I took the bait and volunteered for another good thing to make someone special to me happy.

Isn't this all so wonderful? Aren't I such a nice Christian woman? Isn't the Lord pleased with me? No. Absolutely not! I have been unfaithful to our relationship. I have grieved the Holy Spirit. I have placed others before God. Jesus understands, doesn't He? *"He that loves his son or daughter more than me is not worthy of me" (Matthew 10:37b).* These are hard words, but they are His words to us who have so many good things to do that we neglect seasons of intimacy with the Lover of our souls.

My choices were not between good and bad. My choices were between good and best.

And I made the wrong choice. My wonderful son is ten years old. I did not on that Friday, however, choose the One who came to me when I was ten years old, walking by myself on a Sunday afternoon toward the little Baptist church in our rural community.

As I, that little ten-year-old girl, came near the grove of towering pine trees, just before the Piney Community Cemetery on one side of the road and a wet swampy marsh on the other, sensed a Presence with me that I had never experienced before. It was a presence comparable to what John Wesley called being "strangely warmed" during his salvation experience. Since before I could remember, I was taken to the church and taught the stories of the Bible in Sunday School and Baptist Training Union. They were real to me, but they were not mine.

My own story was comprised of the loving support of my mother and her wonderful family. I had been born to her just after she turned 20 years old. She was not married, and it meant shame and a major change in the life she had planned. Instead of continuing at Jarvis College, she would have a child to raise with very limited economic and social choices. I was totally and carefully embraced by my grandfather, aunts, uncles, and cousins. But deep inside, I could not help but wonder about my father. Why had he rejected me? The drive to have his acceptance and the desire to make my mother proud pushed me to excel in school and in church.

As I looked around the community, I could see how difficult is was for my family to make a living. My grandfather worked on another man's farm, as did other local men. The women, including my mom did "day's work," which meant cleaning houses and taking care of other people's kids. During the sweltering summers, many of the men and women joined forces to pick, pull, and chop hundreds of acres of cotton. The kids helped, too. Meanwhile, on the black and white television screen, I could see other places, far away and inviting. I could see different ways of making a living. I could see lots of things going on in what appeared to be a much larger world. And all the while I was making observations about the world, I kept learning about this God, who I was told loved me so much that He came in the body of Jesus Christ for me.

As I continued slowly up the road toward the church, I could sense that things were not what they seemed. God was present and was present to change things. As I walked, a Power, a Presence rose inside of my body. A voice spoke from within me telling me that it was time for me to receive God for me—for my own life. There was a calm but strong assurance that my life would be very special from then on, that God would always be with me. I was warmed from the inside. That evening after Rev. John W. Williams preached, without consulting anyone, I went forward and gave my young life to Jesus Christ. It was the beginning of an adventure that has been rich and rewarding . . . and painful.

One of the experiences I always looked forward to every year was summer vacation. Since I was the oldest child, early on I became the caretaker for the younger children. Summer vacation was the time we could go to Dallas to spend several weeks with my aunts and uncles who had already relocated there. It was so exciting for me to see the big city and to have increased responsibility. But, I would soon learn that there was increased peril—peril that I had never known or imagined. There was peril that awaited me which would steal my innocence, bring pain and confusion into my life, along with shame and regret.

I had been baby-sitting for several days when a man who claimed to be a "friend" of my aunt dropped by in the middle of the day. I could not understand why he was there since it was clear that my aunt was at work. The man asked where she was and whether any other adults were there. He spoke softly and nervously. He walked slowly into the apartment and took note of the children. Somehow, they ended up playing in the back yard. Confusion enveloped my young life. From the very beginning, I knew that what he called "our secret" was wrong. He said the children would be hurt if I told. Besides all that, what words would I use? Who could I tell? We never talked about that kind of activity in my family. This was a totally foreign concept to me.

Then, there was the matter of God. Hadn't I just weeks before begun a relationship with God in earnest? How could this be happening? The summer could not end soon enough for me, so I could get back home to Piney, to innocence. I studied hard in school, really hard. I worked hard in the church, in the choir, ushering, teaching, helping with the other kids. Maybe there was something I had done wrong. If I could just do everything right from then on, this would not happen again, I reasoned.

I was wrong. The next summer brought the same sinister situation and more guilt and confusion. The harder I tried to run toward God, the more I felt betrayed, maybe by God, but certainly by some of the adults who claimed to be friends of my family. I needed God so much. Where was He? God's real people were all around me. He had put them there. But, I did not share my story, my pain, my horror. Instead, those things would eventually become what would drive me away from the God I loved and who loved me so much that He gave His only Son for me.

When I left home at 17 years of age, I also called myself leaving God and God's people. But, God never left me. God made a way for me to go college, graduate in three years, land my dream job months before graduating, and meet my future husband. God and the Church were such a part of his life that we would go to church together. As I looked back over my life, I began to warm again to the truth that God loves me. I had blamed God for some things that were not God's fault, and I had learned from the Lord that they were not my fault either.

One Sunday morning as my then fiancé and I sat in worship at the historic St. John's Baptist Church in Dallas, I sensed the presence of the Lord as I had as a little girl. The warmth returned. The coldness melted away. Pastor Wilson, after the message, began to sing one of the old hymns my grandfather used to lead us in: "A charge to keep, I have, A God to Glorify."* My heart began to beat for God again, leaping over all the confusion and pain. I ran again into the arms of the Lord, who has been and will always be the great Lover of my soul.

Did I say always? Am I talking about the One who is the same yesterday, today, and forever? Is He not the One who was and is and is to come? Is He not the One who was not surprised by my lack of attention on our special day? The One who even now bids me to come, re-connect and share an intimate time of love and mercy and forgiveness and blessing with Him?

Jesus loves me. It is this Jesus who met me in the bend of the road in Piney almost 38 years ago. This is the One who still speaks ever so gently to me, who cries when I cry, even as He wipes away my tears. My tears this time were because I hurt him. I grieved the Holy Spirit, not by doing the good things I did, but by leaving Him totally out of my plans. It would have been a perfect opportunity for me to have taught my son how to have a Sabbath time with the true and living God.

I have learned the lesson. I hope you will learn from my mistake.

I must go now. He bids me to come to Him.

---

*   *A Charge to Keep I Have,* Words by Charles Wesley, 1762.

                               Yes, Jesus Loves Me

For He will command His angels concerning you
to guard you in all your ways...
"Because he loves me," says the LORD,
"I will rescue him;
I will protect him, for he acknowledges my name.
He will call upon me, and I will answer him;
I will be with him in trouble,
I will deliver him and honor him."
(Psalms 91:11, 14-15)

Anne Clark
was born in Marshallville, GA
and currently resides in Griffin, GA.
She is an elementary school counselor
who believes that her career
is a Divine calling from God.
The year Anne was chosen
"Teacher of the Year,"
the yearbook's dedication to her read,
"Kind, helpful, joyful, dependable.
These words and so many more
describe her! Her smile
and positive attitude
make our school
an enjoyable place to be."
Anne's daily prayer
is that her light will shine
so that others may see
Christ in her.

✝

Anne's Love Story

~≈⊰≈~

Yes, Jesus loves me! I have had an awareness of Him in my life since coming to the realization that I needed air to breathe. My mother, a spirit-filled woman who never ceased to let my siblings and me know that God is in control, was greatly responsible for that. She loved the Lord with all her heart and was not ashamed to share that love and the message of the gospel of Jesus with us or anyone else. Those early teachings of my mother, no doubt, prepared me for some hardships, many of which, perhaps, I would not have been able to endure.

Although it seems that I've always known the Lord, I have come to realize that knowing and having a personal relationship with Him are two different things. It's like the difference between dating and marriage; you know the person you're dating, but you don't really "know" him until you've entered into that committed relationship with him—until you've been through something together. My earlier knowledge of God had been based on my mother's accounts of the Gospel and her recitations of scripture, the picture of Jesus on our living room wall, the lessons I'd been taught about Him at the church and Sunday School I attended, and the visions of Him that came to me in my dreams. When I was a child, I would often dream about Jesus and heaven.

Such knowledge, along with my mother's love and faith, sustained me through my childhood in the home of an alcoholic and abusive father and into my young adulthood.

After I'd been out of school and working for a while, I started thinking about settling down. I started looking for "Mr. Right." I would petition God daily for my life partner. There was a void in my life that I thought could only be filled by a husband. I asked God to send me someone who would love Him first, but who would love me as much as I loved him. Then, my prayers were answered, or so I thought. The man that came into my life was nice, liked the nicer things in life, was educated, had a good job. He, too, was churched. I had met him in graduate school years before. Although he had asked me out several times, because we lived in different cities and for other reasons, we had never been able to get together.

Then, I called him one day and suggested we go to a play together. One date led to another and another, and before I knew it we were making wedding plans. We married the following spring. I moved to his city and started attending his church. After a short while I joined his church and was again united with a wonderful body of believers. Ah, we had made that church connection; we regularly went to church and Sunday school together. Even with such a connection, there was something missing in our lives. After a year or so into our marriage, my husband never seemed to have much time for me anymore. If he had a list of things to do, it was almost a guarantee I was going to be on the bottom of the list. When we were dating, he would go to church and Sunday School with me every Sunday, but he began to gradually pull away from the church and from me. I would ignore some of the signs and refused to believe that his negligence of our marriage could ever end up in divorce court. I would tell myself, "God, you gave me this man and our marriage. I made a commitment to him and a vow to you, and I'm going to hang in there."

I think my husband felt guilty leaving me home alone so much, so he encouraged me to return to school and get another degree. My response to that was, "School! Are you out of your mind?" But he kept encouraging me and saying things like, "You are too smart not to continue with your education." Finally, I decided to follow his suggestions. I was accepted in postgraduate school and started attending school the spring of the next year.

A year later, I received my third professional degree, but my marriage was no better for it. Instead of things getting better, they got worse. My husband was spending more and more time away from home. He decided to go back to school for a fourth degree, and this he pursued in another state, which put even more distance between us. He was gone almost every weekend, as well as every summer. He would compensate for not being home by sending beautiful flowers to my job. He took me to elegant hotels on special occasions, such as our anniversaries and my birthdays. He also bought us a beautiful house in an upscale community. But it became more and more apparent to me that the flowers, the outings, even the house were all for appearance's sake and not for love's sake.

He gave me a lot of material things, but he did not give of himself, the one thing I wanted the most. I knew our marriage needed a lot of work, and since I loved my husband, I decided I was going to do everything within my power to make it work. I still refused to entertain the notion of leaving him, because, after all, I had prayed for him, and God had sent him as an answer to my prayers. I would often ask God for His guidance. I truly wanted us to work things out. I even suggested a counselor, but to no avail.

Finally in the summer of our fifth year of being together, things began to come unglued in our marriage. Late one night in

July, while my husband was attending school in another state, I got a devastating telephone call. I could not believe what I was hearing. My husband . . . unfaithful! I didn't want to believe the caller. I had always trusted my husband. I got up and began searching the house for clues to these accusations. In my heart, I hoped to find none so that the caller could be disproved. I couldn't find anything. Good! Then, I sat in a chair and asked God to direct me. I told Him I did not want to be used, and if it was His will for me to know what was going on, to please show it to me. Immediately, He sent me to the trash can and I found the evidence I had hoped I wouldn't find. I called my husband the next day and told him every thing that had happened. He came home that night to pacify me and assure me that things were going to be all right. That assurance that things were going to be "all right" led me to believe he wanted to work things out, but that was not the case.

I started to find more evidence of his unfaithfulness. I grew increasingly distrustful of him. He grew angrier with me for searching through his things and for questioning him when he left the house, something I had never done before. In the face of all this, I still refused to give up on this man that had been answered prayer to me. I prayed and read the Bible a lot, asking God to help us work things out. God had answered me before, surely He would answer this plea, as well. I thought things would get better but they didn't. Where was God now? I began to feel abandoned by God.

Then, I began to wonder, "What have I done to deserve this travesty in my marriage?" Surely, I must have done something to bring about this situation. I asked God to show me the things I had done wrong, and I began to plead with Him, that if I had not been a Godly wife to forgive me of my shortcomings.

Despite my protests and pleadings to God, despite my desires that my marriage be saved, the dreaded words came from my husband on a Sunday night in August that same summer. "We don't belong together." I couldn't believe it. I didn't want to believe it.

Then he told me all I needed to do was heed my own words, spoken to a church audience that very morning, "God will take care of you." Things happened quickly after that. Within three weeks, he saw a lawyer and had divorce papers drawn up—papers he handed me one morning while I sat at the counter reading a meditation, preparing to go to school and interact with students. I couldn't believe it! I was given divorce papers and had to go to work in the next twenty minutes! I was angry and hurt. I didn't know what to do. Should I go to work or stay home and call in sick? I decided I would probably do better if I went to work and was around people. Staying at home would have depressed me even more.

Once I got to school, again, I didn't know what to do. I had fifteen minutes to collect myself before the school day began. At 8:02, two minutes after the official start of the day, a little first grader walked in my office, gave me a hug and said, "I love you." It was quiet in the midst of the storm. It was a still small voice. It was the voice of God. I knew, then, why God wanted me at work. While sitting in my office by myself contemplating all the things that had transpired that morning, a group of students walked in my office, gave me hugs and said they loved me, too. I felt the Presence of the Holy Spirit. A day that had started out so wretched, ended up being a wonderful day.

I had got an audible "I love you" from God that morning, spoken through a child.

> *I love the Lord, for he heard my voice; he heard my cry for mercy. Because he turned his ear to me, I will call on him as long as I live . . . I was overcome by trouble and sorrow. Then I called on the name of the Lord: "O Lord, save me!" The Lord is gracious and righteous; our God is full of compassion. The Lord protects the simple hearted; when I was in great need, He saved me" (Psalms 116:1-6).*

From the earliest hours following being served with my divorce papers, God began to show His love in extraordinary ways. I had been stripped of all the things that had provided me with security in the past—my mother's prayers and my husband's protection. I could not even feel the security that the church had always provided. This was the first time in my life that I was truly "alone." I had no one to rely on, but God. For the first time, I had to go to seek Him, not only for things of comfort and pleasure, not just for the provision of things and people to make me happy and fill voids in my life, but I had to depend on Him for life. When I look back over all the things that happened to me, I know that nothing was an accident. These things were proof of God's love for me.

What my husband said to me on that Sunday night, one of the worst nights in my life, proved to be true, "God will take care of you." And He did. He took care of me through a near-fatal car accident; He provided for me during a financially stressful time, so that I wouldn't miss even one mortgage payment. He carried me when I had no strength and little will to carry on. He sent me angels with words of comfort and encouragement, with rides when I was without a car. His angels supplied whatever was needed. *"For he will command his angels concerning you to guard you in all your ways" (Psalms 91:11)*. I have come into a new knowledge, a true knowledge of God and His love for me. He is an ever-present help in the time of trouble. He is the supplier of all my needs. He is the lover of my soul. Yes, Jesus loves me, and this I truly know!

"For I know the plans I have for you,"
declares the Lord,
"plans to prosper you and not to harm you,
plans to give you hope and a future."
(Jeremiah 29:11)

Jeanette Clift George
is the founder and Artistic Director
of the A.D. Players,
the Houston-based
Christian Theater Company
which offers plays throughout the world.
Jeanette is equally well-known as author,
playwright, Bible teacher, and national speaker.
In her radio program,
"Jeanette Clift George from Center Stage,"
her unique wit and keen insights
illuminate Biblical principles.
She is author of the books,
Daisy Petals,
Travel Tips From a Reluctant Traveler, and
Some Run With Feet of Clay
offered through her publishing company,
Manor of Grace.

†

Day **25**

Jeanette's Love Story

～≈≈～

It was a small thing—this unscheduled epiphany. One of
many interruptions of God in my life. I was a Believer, newly restored to Christ through recognition of His Lordship after a time
spent in idle Christianity and open rebellion. I was working in theater in New York. Christian fellowship was hard to find in the day-
to-day communion with fellow theater workers. Theater was the
only religion I had served and respected, and I felt out of place in
the new world of faith in God. I was on my way to an interview for
a job when a sudden rain stopped me. Seeking shelter, I stood under the awning of a bookstore. When they rolled up the awning, I
asked if there was a place for me to stay until the storm diminished.
The bookstore owner told me I would be welcome at a service being held in a small chapel above the bookstore. I was not interested
in attending a chapel service, but was eager to stay out of the rainstorm, so, I perched on the back pew for a meeting held over the
bookstore. I never put down my purse or took off my coat—I only
meant to stay for the few minutes of the storm.

The speaker was Major Ian Thomas. He spoke of Abraham, who, when called, obeyed—not knowing where he was going. I had never heard that before, and the principle presented in Major Thomas' precise British accent held my attention. And, then, Major Thomas said that to follow God, Abraham had to pack. Packing was something I did as an actress going to jobs in various theaters. For the first time, I identified with the activity of a Bible character and found it personally relevant. There was, first of all, the principle of Abraham's faith—I saw myself obeying God in the scant information I had of the future. Still balanced on the arm of the back pew, I also saw another principle; I saw the drama of the Bible enacted in the visuals of my mind. And, I saw the option of theater under the authority of the Living God—and there was a place for me.

Today I am the full-time Artistic Director of a Christian Theater company, with 35 years of active history and 38 full-time personnel. I am an actress, a director and a playwright for whom God personally directed a New York City rainstorm, the closing hours of a bookstore, an appointed speaker, and an hour set apart for a life-changing principle. In the energy of faith, I can trust in the God Who personalized His Sovereign Power to enter my life with the assurance of His Love, His Lordship and His intimate Leadership. *"Those who know your name will trust in you, for you, Lord, have never forsaken those who seek you"* (Psalms 9:10).

Sing, O Daughter of Zion;
shout aloud, O Israel!
Be glad and rejoice with all your heart,
O Daughter of Jerusalem!
The LORD your God is with you,
He is mighty to save.
He will take great delight in you,
He will quiet you with His love,
He will rejoice over you with singing.
(Zephaniah 3:14, 17)

Jewel E. Smith
accepted Jesus Christ
as her Lord and Savior
at the age of eleven.
She continues to seek His will,
walk in faith and mature spiritually.
Jewel is married to James W.,
and they have two wonderful daughters,
J'Mill and Jennerette.
Jewel's prayer for people
around the world is that
eyes will be opened to recognize
the King of Kings and
that Jesus will be accepted
as God's Son and
the only free gift of salvation.

✝

Day **26**

Jewel's Love Story

〜〜

"I come to the garden alone,
While the dew is still on the roses;
And the voice I hear,
Falling on my ear;
The Son of God discloses.
And He walks with me, and He talks with me,
And He tells me I am His own,
And the joy we share as we tarry there,
None other has ever known."
—C. Austin Miles, 1912

I have been taught about the sustaining love of God through a long line of God-fearing, God-believing family members. Yet, I did not comprehend such love. And though I knew I had often been delivered from troubles, worries, fears, family matters, sickness, work concerns, financial disasters, over-commitment of time, and a host of other circumstances from which I was in need of deliverance, I did not recognize these things as any acts of love. Perhaps I just thought it was God being God—you know, doing what God is supposed to do. What did love have to do with it?

That was pretty much my mindset until about five years ago. It was then that the Holy Spirit began drawing me, hinting that there was something more. Until then I had been pretty comfortable just being "a sinner saved by grace," reaping the benefits, and sharing a few testimonies here and there about God's goodness and other benefits of being that saved sinner. After the testimonies were done, it was back to my daily routine, with no real yearning to know God and His love or to spend time with Him. You see, I could turn God on or off, at will. And I pretty much did. That way of responding to Him, however, became no longer enough. It was not enough for me. It was clearly not enough for Him. There was first of all the feeling that something was missing, then the trying to fill that feeling with stuff and activity. And when I had filled much of my time, I still had a yearning. The answer would come that what I lacked was a relationship with God.

Approximately five years ago, The Holy Spirit moved on a small group of ladies from my church to form an early Saturday morning prayer time. We were bathed and nourished spiritually and began a transforming journey. It is amazing how our spirits at times united with the heartbeat of God. Our journey took us through various stages of growth. In our earliest stage, we were "His Girls," followed by Watchmen On the Wall, Women of Faith, and finally, His Bride. It was somewhere between the Women of Faith and His Bride stage that my inner spirit panted for a deeper love relationship with the Most High.

The early Saturday morning hours spent with Him were treasured and anticipated and left me wanting more! The Holy Spirit's response to me was that I could not only come to the garden occasionally, but I could be in the garden with the Lover of my Soul all the time. What I needed to fill the emptiness I felt was not an occasional encounter with God, but a relationship with Him. That was the something more that I had been looking for.

What is a love relationship with the King of the Universe? It is abiding in God and God abiding in me. Abiding is not about coming and going. It is not about keeping company with Him sometimes. It is about coming and staying. About taking up residence within—permanent residence. What I learned through the Holy Spirit's teaching is that when you abide in the King and He in you, you are plugged into His perfect love for eternity. No one or thing can pluck you out of that blessed assurance. I recently attended an IMAX™ showing of a documentary on the climbing of Mt. Kilamanjaro in Africa. The documentary showed a unique type of tree that grows on the mountain whose leaves never fall off. When its season as a leaf is complete, the leaf clings to the tree until it is grafted into the tree! Like the leaf in that tree, I abide in Him and He in me.

(Song)
I'm just abiding in the tree
I'm just abiding in the tree
Abiding in the tree
Abiding in the tree
I'm just abiding in the tree

What is a love relationship with my Lord? It is the total surrender of my self and my desires to Him, so that I can give attention and action to the things that please my Lord—my Beloved. "Lord, what pleases you today?" I have asked in times of intimacy with Him. Sometimes He desires confession and repentance; sometimes He would have me bless Him with song, dance, exhortation, journaling, or just a holy awe and quietness. But, He answers.

(Song)
Beep, Beep, Holy Beep, Beep
Beep, Beep, Holy Beep, Beep
Beep, Beep, Holy Beep, Beep
Got a Holy Beep, Beep in my soul.

What is a love relationship with my Abba, Father? It is taking Him at His Word. Believing Him. Believing in Him. Trusting Him. When you finally get it and you know He loves you and that you love Him, you can rest in the fact that no harm will come to you and that all things are working together for your good. When I realize that the God of all creation is my ever-present help in times of trouble and that He is my Father who will provide all that I need according to His riches in glory, how can I not love Him? How can I not trust Him?

(Song)
Not by sight
Not by sound
Not by what I feel
Not by circumstances
I walk by faith

What is a love relationship with The Great I Am? It is having intimate fellowship with Him. It is talking to Him—often. It my hearing Him when He speaks to me. It is listening. Hearing His voice in whatever way He speaks. It is having Him reveal Himself and His tender mercies to me in all that surrounds me. It is my standing in awe of such revelations. When I was vacationing with my family in Hawaii a few years ago, I went snorkeling for the first time in the Pacific Ocean. As I floated effortlessly below the waters, I was awestruck by the beauty and vastness of the work of God's hands. Tears still cascade down my cheeks as I ponder the love He demonstrates through His beautiful creations. He speaks. How beautiful He must be to behold! One day I asked God, "God, how old are you?" He answered me, "I am forever new." He speaks to me. Scripture tells us that He is the "Great I Am," the Alpha and Omega, the One who was and is and is to come—worthy to receive honor and power and blessings, the One who speaks with thunder and lightning; yet He speaks into my heart His whispers of love for me.

(Song)
My heart is filled
With nothing else but you my King
There is no room, no room for any other thing
I give my heart completely
And follow after you, cause I love you, Lord
I really, really, do.

In any love relationship, however, the time comes when you long to know just what you mean to your beloved, just who you are to him. The time came when I longed to know. Less than a year ago, I felt compelled to ask God, "Just who am I to you?" His response was, "You are my Child of Song."

He had called me by name. He had called me by a new name that He had especially for me—a name that spoke of my purpose and what I meant to Him! And the Holy Spirit spoke to me, *"And you will sing as on the night you celebrate a holy festival; your hearts will rejoice as when people go up with flutes to the mountain of the Lord, to the Rock of Israel"* (Isaiah 30:29).

How that blessed my heart! I suppose that's when I got it! When I finally got it! When He called me by name. In His calling me by name, I came to know that I am special to Him. I came to know that, yes, He loves me! Since that time, I have been filled with song. Why, I can even remember waking up from sleeping with songs in my consciousness that I must have been singing in my sleep. The only times I remember composing songs prior to this time were once with my sister during childhood and during each pregnancy while I waited with thankful heart to give birth to my two wonderful daughters. Now, during my times with God, I capture on paper the songs that flow from my heart to His. I have shared the first verse of those songs that have welled up in my spirit at different times since God shared my special name with me.

And through my new name, my kinship to the Father was further realized, for He, too, sings over His children. *"On that day they will say to Jerusalem, Do not fear, O Zion; do not let your hands hang limp. The Lord your God is with you . . . He will quiet you with His love, He will rejoice over you with singing"* *(Zephaniah 3:16-17).*

Praise be to the God and Father of our Lord Jesus Christ,
the Father of compassion and the God of all comfort,
Who comforts us in all our troubles,
so that we can comfort those in any trouble
with the comfort we ourselves have received from God.
(2 Corinthians 1:3-4)

Vyonne Carter-Johnson
is a wife of 30 years,
a mother, a daughter and
a career-oriented woman.
Vyonne tries to live out her
Christian values in the workplace
as well as in private.
She is a cancer survivor who shares
her story with the community.
"Every day I thank God
for His constant presence,"
Vyonne says.
"I daily thank Him for my husband,
son and mother,
because I believe all things are possible
as long as I have this loving God
and this loving community of
friends and family."

✝

Day 27

Vyonne's Love Story

≋≋

"My Father's Love"

God prepares me for all the crosses I must bear. Whether I know it or not, I am being prepared just the same. Sometimes I have to look back—sometimes even a few years back—in order to see that the road I just traveled had already been paved with God's love and grace. July 12, 1985 was just such a day.

In late spring-early summer of 1983, after many years of only attending church when I went home to New Orleans, I experienced an all-consuming need to become a regular, card-carrying, every-Sunday church member. I had driven past the church I currently attend, St. George's and St. Patrick's, at least three times a week with little notice of it. Then, one day "out-of-the-blue," as if it had been put there just for me, I noticed it. I noticed first that it was a church, and second that it was an Episcopal Church. It was like I had found my home.

My life in church grew in God's love and grace with no significant ups and downs that I can remember until 1984. In September of that year, my father decided he would, for the first time, visit us in Houston where we had lived since 1972. He visited for about a week. During the visit, my father seemed to have a pressing need to tell me all he could about who he was and what his life experiences had been. In essence, he had a need to tell me what in life had helped shape him into the man he became. Some stories were funny, some mundane, some very serious, and some sad. Many had a lasting effect on me. We had a visit that was filled with love, joy, laughter, and sharing.

Then, in October, my father told me of some pain he was experiencing. He said that the doctors thought it might be muscle spasms or a pulled muscle, but that it was certainly nothing to worry about. They gave him a muscle relaxer and an aspirin-type pain medication. The pain did not go away, nor did it decrease. His pain actually got worse.

In November, the doctors performed exploratory surgery. He came out of the surgery just fine; however, the diagnosis was a Pancos tumor, lung cancer, which would have to be removed. That was fine, we would deal with it. His doctor scheduled the surgery, removed the tumor, and scheduled chemo and radiation therapy.

Christmas time. I went home, and during my visit, my father told me that when he felt better he would have to find a church to attend. He said he'd thought, "It is time for me to make peace with my Maker." There was significance in that statement, because in 34 years, I had never seen my father in a church for any reason—not for weddings, funerals, baptisms, not even my confirmation or my brother's confirmation—not for anything. That was the first time I felt a sense of peace with my father's disease. God was with him.

My father continued treatments. Since October, he had been in constant, escalating pain. I had to learn to live with my sense of guilt at not being able to be with him all the time. I could not be there to visit or see him daily or even every other day. I prayed and, lovingly, God provided. Between Christmas and July, with the love and financial support from several people in my life, I flew every other weekend to New Orleans, with the exception of one weekend when my husband and I drove. My husband and I paid; my best friend paid; my stepfather and my mother, who had been divorced from my father for 15 years, paid for some of the trips.

Then, sometime in May, I felt that my father would not be alive much longer. I cried, felt guilty, moaned, and groaned about how I could not do more for my father. With God's help, however, I began to understand that I had done all I could do and that this was all God was asking of me. He would take care of the rest.

On July 11, while my husband and I were on vacation, my stepmother called and said the doctor said to come now. She said, "Your father is in a coma and is not expected to live." We packed and left for New Orleans. We arrived in New Orleans at about 2 a.m., decided to get some sleep, get up at 6 a.m., and go to the hospital. The next morning at about 6:30 a.m., my stepmother called to say my father had just died.

I was stunned, then angry, and then at peace. Before the peace came, however, it dawned on me that no hospital in the country would have stopped me from going to see my dying father at 2 a.m., had I requested it. But, I did not think of going to see him at that time. We only thought of going to see him at 6 a.m. The fact that this didn't occur to me at 2 a.m., I later concluded, indicated that I was not supposed to be there any sooner than I was. If I were supposed to have been there in the hospital any sooner, then certainly, I would have known it at that time. It was not my doing. It was God's doing.

During the next few days, I looked deep into my heart to reflect, search, and discern what I really felt about the dying and death of my father. The conclusion was—my father is at peace. Introspection revealed that I could accept his dying and his death, while remembering to appreciate the time God had given us. Without God paving the road all those months before, I do not know how I would have felt. Without question, I was a "Daddy's Girl." The sun rose and set with my father. Though he was a man of many faults, I always held a special place in his heart and he in mine. Until my father died, I had a fear of death a mile wide and a world deep. Never in my 34 years had I even attended a funeral.

My father died on July 12, 1985. That was the first true test of my adult beliefs in God. The death of my father was a sad time in my life, but during the months he was dying, he and I both "walked" a little closer to each other and to the Lord. And, surprisingly, during one of the saddest occasions of my life, God revealed His love to me. He did so by preparing my father to go to His heavenly home and by preparing my heart as well. He did so by giving me grace to overcome my own fear of death and to come to see it as the natural progression of life that it is. He did so by granting me peace and understanding to accept the death of my earthly father and the death of all loved ones. This understanding does not take away the feeling of loss or of missing the individual, but what it does do for me is to make death an inevitable part of life and, thus, acceptable. I can now visualize the loved one with God in his Kingdom, as I know my father is. Through a well-orchestrated series of events, shaped by the hands of a loving Heavenly Father, my earthly father's death was sad, but it was not the traumatic time it could have been. I truly believed then, as I believe now, that he is at peace.

Just as Jesus has made His love for me known, I now can return this love by using one of the gifts God has given me. Through God, I have become a very able layreader. I use this gift by serving in church and at funeral and burial services. As God ministered to me in my time of grief, He allows me to minister to others who are grieving. I look upon this ministry as a gift, not only to the grieving family, but also as a last gift to the departed.

My Father in heaven has granted peace and understanding when I think of my earthly father. It is the love of Jesus that gives me peace to accept gracefully the death of my loved ones. In good times and in bad times, I know God is with me and I am loved. And because God loves me, and I love God, one day, I will be with Him in paradise.

God is love!

Your loving daughter, *Vyonne*

You will seek Me and find Me
when you seek Me with all your heart.
(Jeremiah 29:13)

Sheila Starks Phillips
is a native Texan
who has been
telling stories professionally since 1990.
A former first grade teacher and
zookeeper at the Houston Zoo,
Sheila performs around the country
sharing her stories of wit and wisdom.
Sheila plays guitar and sings in a music group
at her church
called the POGS (People of God).
She is also on the
Traveling Artists Roster of the
Texas Commission on the Arts.

✝

Day 28

Sheila's Love Story

"God is so Good . . . all the Time!"

I have been a churchgoer my entire life. Although my family often had a tendency to drop the kids at Sunday School and then go home, still we all attended church on a fairly regular basis together. However, we were not a *praying family*. At Thanksgiving, when it would seem right and proper to pray together before cutting that big old turkey, it was extremely awkward because we never prayed together any other time of the year.

It was only after I was an adult, married with three children, that I came to realize that there was much more to this being a Christian and believing in our Lord Jesus Christ than just going to church on Sundays.

Our church had a "Faith Alive" weekend. A whole new concept for most of us. A team of people came from other cities to glorify the Lord. There was much singing of praise songs and personal witnessing. My family hosted some of the team members, and we also hosted one of the neighborhood coffees. As individual team members described their walk with God, I was dumbstruck. I had never heard anyone speak of a personal relationship with God. At first, I was skeptical, and then I was overwhelmed with a desire to have that kind of relationship for myself.

After the weekend, I could think of little else. I read my Bible like I had never read it before. I talked incessantly to other believers. Then, one day as I was driving down the streets of Houston, I was overcome with emotion and began to sob uncontrollably. I wasn't sad or despondent in any way. In fact, I was overjoyed and so full of love that all I could do was cry. I turned my car around and drove straight to our church to talk to our priest. I was not at all sure I wasn't going off the deep end. He explained to me that I had indeed been filled with the Holy Spirit. What a joyous moment! We prayed together thanking God for this incredible blessing and for His love.

"Jesus replied, 'If anyone loves me, he will obey my teaching. My Father will love him, and we will come to him and make our home with him'" (John 14:23).

About six months after that experience, a time when I was growing ever stronger in my faith with each step I took in my walk with God, my youngest son, who had just turned fifteen, broke his neck during a football game. We were told initially that he would be paralyzed for life and never walk again. We began to pray, asking God to heal this child and make him whole again. Through two surgeries and many months of hospitalization and rehabilitation, he did walk again, and today is strong and whole.

Throughout the entire ordeal, I could feel the love of God surrounding, not only me, but our whole family. Never once was I disheartened. Never once did I feel abandoned by God. I could feel His presence in those hospital rooms. I could feel the Holy Spirit lifting me up as we dealt with each new situation. I felt an incredible peace throughout because I knew God was with me. *"Peace I leave with you; my peace I give you . . ."* *(John 14:27).* We were surrounded by loving friends and family and by the love of our Lord. We knew, absolutely knew, God was there with us and would always be there with us regardless of the outcome. And He has been.

God is so good . . . all the time!

When you pass through the waters,
I will be with you;
and when you pass through the rivers,
they will not sweep over you.
When you walk through the fire,
you will not be burned;
the flames will not set you ablaze.
For I am the LORD, your God...
(Isaiah 43:2-3)

Clara Knight
was born and raised in
Kansas City, MO and is a
graduate of the University of Iowa.
God blessed her with two sons,
Alex and Jordan.
In Grandview, MO where she currently resides,
Clara is active in the
Palestine Missionary Baptist Church
of Jesus Christ serving as
Sunday School teacher, usher
and counselor to junior ushers,
and member of the Cherished Sisterhood Ministry.
She volunteers for Youth Friends,
a mentoring program for students
in the Raytown School District
and is a member of
Delta Sigma Theta Sorority.

✝

Day *29*

Clara's Love Story

‿‿

God's love is powerful. When I should have been otherwise drowning, sinking, or lost in despair, His love absolutely engulfed and kept me.

A mother's love is strong and symbolic, enduring and everlasting. Yet has anyone ever measured the depth of a mother's pain? I have. Few things can break a mother's bond with her child. Death ranks at the top of my list, visiting October 1, 1996. How do you prepare to say goodbye to your first born when your day started with a visit to the emergency room? Would I have done things differently had I known that day was our last? Probably. Maybe. No. I'm just not sure.

The same God who allowed the pain in my heart that morning also calmed the raging nightmare of loss, suffering, and crying by providing peace in the midst of my storm. You see, my son Alex was just nine years old when God took him. He confessed Christ as His Lord and Savior at the age of seven believing that He died for our sins. Now that God had called him home, why would I stand in the way of His work? After all, isn't that part of being a Christian, so that we can see Heaven?

I knew Alex was sick, yet I didn't know it would result in his death that day. He had Scleroderma, a rare skin disease that leads to death. In the hospital room, I felt God's presence. I knew He was with us, but I didn't know it was because He was claiming His child. I stayed in constant prayer, asking for healing grace for Alex. Even though God heard my plea, my earthly request was denied. I left the hospital without my son, and that night I cried myself to sleep.

I didn't have any doubt because I knew He would take care of me. I prayed for strength and peace of mind for my journey. I can't explain it, but what I experienced the next day few days was similar to the peace Paul talks about in Philippians—the kind of peace "which transcends all understanding." I calmly made funeral arrangements. God carried me every step of the way, showing me His true love. During Alex's funeral, I was able to greet family and friends with a warm loving smile. You see it was God's arms supporting me, helping me to stand when I should have fallen.

That day, I did not feel like a mother who had lost her child but like a child of God being cared for by her Heavenly Father. A sweet holy spirit was flowing within me, allowing me to bury my son while knowing someday I would see him again. After Alex's funeral, I was convinced then as I am now, that nothing short of God's grace and love carried me. How else can I explain functioning when most would falter?

In Mary Stevenson's poem, "Footprints in the Sand," she says, "During the low periods of my life when I was suffering from anguish, sorrow, or defeat, I could see only one set of footprints." When asked about this, the Lord replies, "The times when you have seen only one set of footprints are when I carried you."*

One set of footprints was left for me that week in October of 1996. Yet again and again, I've never walked alone. Do I know that Jesus loves me? I am convinced more than ever that He does.

* *Footprints in the Sand*, Written by Mary Stevenson in 1936, copyright 1984.

The Lord longs to be gracious to you;
He rises to show you compassion.
(Isaiah 30:18)

Lois Wilson
is a pastor, teacher, writer, storyteller,
and artist who lives in Philadelphia
with her husband and their five children.
She is a graduate of
Eastern Baptist Theological Seminary and
is currently enrolled in the D. Th. Program
at the University of South Africa.
Lois has served the Philadelphia community
as a childbirth educator and
home-birth midwife from 1988-2000.
She now serves as Pastoral Assistant
at First Baptist Church in Browns Mills, NJ,
as well as developing
an itinerant ministry (Servant's Heart Ministries)
offering retreats and workshops on
Biblical storytelling, sacred dance
and Christian Ritual Art.

✝

Lois' Love Story

It all began two years earlier. I was wounded by our former church. A deep wound. So deep, in fact, that I walked away from God, church, and Christianity. I hadn't opened my Bible in two years. I hadn't prayed. I was bitter and defiant. I didn't need God.

It was during this time that I began to teach natural childbirth classes in our little row house in Philadelphia. Every week our tiny living room was filled with pregnant women and their partners. We laughed and ate and shared our stories. Friendships formed. Trust bloomed. And many of them invited me to attend their births.

One by one the babies came, and a strange thing happened. As each tiny life emerged into the world, I found myself weeping silent tears of pure worship. My heart betrayed me! Against my will, I was worshipping God. With heart-breaking clarity, I recognized it: the sweet sense of awe and adoration, the blunt acknowledgment that God is God.

Time and again waves of worship washed over me in the birth room, until finally I could run from God no more.

"You win," I told God. "My heart and my spirit continue to adore you, even when my will defies you!"

And so I slowly turned to face God again, compelled by a Love that would not let me go. From that point on I have known something that I never really knew before: that I belong to God, and that this fact will never change. I know that God loves me even at my worst, and that nothing I can do will turn His love away. Even when I was running in the opposite direction, angry and bitter, the Lord still loved me! Nothing can remove from my heart the indwelling Spirit's witness, the mark of God's ownership upon my soul, the fact of God's abiding presence and love. His love outlasts our rebellion and sin. Praise His Name!!!

> *For I am convinced that neither death nor life, neither angels nor demons, neither the present nor the future, nor any powers, neither height nor depth, nor anything else in all creation, will be able to separate us from the love of God that is in Christ Jesus our Lord.*
>
> *(Romans 8:38-39)*

He reached down from on high and took hold of me;
He drew me out of deep waters.
He rescued me from my powerful enemy,
from my foes, who were too strong for me.
He brought me out into a spacious place;
He rescued me because He delighted in me.
(Psalms 18:16-17,19)

Kathy Hood Culmer
is a graduate of Spelman College
and the University of South Florida.
She is a teacher and a writer.
Additionally, Kathy has been a
professional storyteller
for the past twelve years,
sharing with audiences ranging from
toddlers through seniors,
always with the desire to teach, to
entertain, and to inspire.
Yes, Jesus Loves Me is the first in her
"Month of Sunday Stories" series.
Kathy and husband, John, have three
daughters and one granddaughter.
They reside in Kingwood, Texas.

✝

Day 31

Kathy's Love Story

It seems that I have spent much of my life seeking the approval, acceptance, and love of somebody. It seems. Early on in my life, it was the seeking of these validations from my peers. Then, when I either recognized the impossibility of succeeding or simply got tired from trying, I began to seek those things from God.

It started out as an unconscious thing. I felt myself being drawn to God. I had grown up in the church, spent much time there, studied many a Sunday School lesson, and served in different capacities, which resulted in my having a pretty good working "head-knowledge" of God. But then, that didn't seem to be enough any more. I don't know whether I sought God out of love for Him, a need for Him, or simply out of a vague familiarity with Him, or because I was so tired and disappointed from seeking those responses from people that I thought my chances were better or easier with Him. After all, He was God. God would not reject me; surely He could not reject that which He Himself had made.

So, my response to this "drawing" to God was the same as it

had been to my need for the love, acceptance, and approval from others: to go in pursuit of the relationship. I pursued it through Bible study. I pursued it by trying to follow the examples of other "Godly" people, who seemed to enjoy God's favor and who were faith-filled, patterning my public behavior, my parenting, and my conversation after theirs. I reasoned that they were "highly favored" by God; their behavior must have been love-worthy to God; therefore, they were good models to follow. For years, I did this. And though God blessed me tremendously over these years, those blessings too often went unacknowledged or "under-acknowledged" because I was looking for a certain manifestation of His love.

Somewhere along the way, after all of my futile attempts to get that manifestation of God's love from Him, after all those years of Bible study and "patterning" my behavior after other Christians and then imposing those values in my home upon my children and my husband, and after all of my pleading and crying before Him to "show me His love" and to "let me feel His love," I must have, somewhere along the way, concluded that God's love and approval and acceptance must be as elusive as the world's.

Through all of this crying, begging, pleading, and feeling rejected by God, I was missing the evidence He had already given me. I was waiting and looking for a profound demonstration of His love. I was looking perhaps for a "Damascus Road" experience where God would knock me out cold and, after I regained consciousness, I would get up feeling loved and ready to do a great work for God. After all, that's how it happened for Paul. Or perhaps I was looking to "hear" the unmistakable, tender, and loving voice of God telling me of His love for me. He does speak to people, you know. Since I didn't hear Him or see Him, then maybe He'd do some really special thing for me that was for me and me alone. Perhaps He would show me His love in some supernatural way. I longed so for His love that I would have taken any of these experiences as proof that He loved me—personally. Then, I would get tired of trying to get it—and weary of not getting it. I would cry out to Him some more. I would question, "What's wrong with me?" I would feel rejected—even by God. Then, when I'd get my strength back, I would start all over again. It has been an exhausting experience.

But, the trouble wasn't with God. Of course, it wasn't. The trouble was with my "looking" for His love. The trouble was with my expectations of what that love looks and sounds and feels like and how it manifests itself. The trouble was that my looking had actually kept me from seeing. Or, perhaps more accurately, my looking had gotten in the way of my recognizing and accepting the demonstrations of love He had already provided.

The "Damascus Road" experience I was hoping for turned out to be more of an "Emmaus Road" experience: *"Now that same day two of them were going to a village called Emmaus, about seven miles from Jerusalem. They were talking with each other about everything that had happened. As they talked and discussed these things with each other, Jesus himself came up and walked along with them; but they were kept from recognizing him"* (Luke 24:13-15). They continued this journey walking and talking with Jesus without ever recognizing Him until— *"When he was at the table with them, he took bread, gave thanks, broke it and began to give it to them. Then their eyes were opened and they recognized him"* (Luke 24:30-31).

God finally gave me a once-and-for-all response to my years of pleading with Him to show me His love, not in any of the anticipated ways, but by giving me an assignment. I didn't even fully get the irony of the assignment until recently, more than a year into the completion of it. God assigned me the task of putting together a collection of 31 stories from women who know God's love personally, wherein they tell of how they came into the knowledge of that love.

The assignment was given to me—of all people—the one who until the very moments I am writing these words, was not sure of my own story. This certainly was not what I had sought as a response from Him, was not a familiar demonstration based on the evidence I had seen in other people's lives; yet this was the response given me. It is only now, as I write these words, that I finally and fully "get it." God's love, though universal because it is available to us all, is also so very personal that the very experience by which He brings us into the knowledge of it is uniquely designed for each of us.

Once I got past the cloudiness created by trying to win His love and prescribing ways in which He could reveal it to me, I was able to see more clearly those demonstrations He had already given. I could then see that those three extra years He gave me with my mother rather than take her away suddenly, thereby sparing me the pain and anguish that I had seen her suffer when her own mother was taken away without warning, was because of His love for me—personally. It was the very special *gift*. That Saturday morning when I was taking a walk and heard words spoken from my heart that said, "Though this life be ill begot, I will still bless this life and purpose it to be for Me," was surely a whisper of His love and assurance. It was the *hearing*.

He has manifested Himself and His love to me through the very dear friend who is there to pray with me and encourage me, telling me often of how much He loves me and challenging me always to believe God for "big things"—to believe Him for everything. Even coming to the realization that what I do and always have done is to speak and write and that this is what He made me to do and is what I will do for Him—even this was an expression of His love. It was my own Damascus Road. But the unveiling—the unveiling of my eyes and sensibilities to see and realize and experience fully His love for me—has come through the calling to and fulfilling of this assignment and from the providing of the necessary people and resources to compile this collection of stories. It was the *supernatural!*

With the cloud lifted I could see and see clearly that God had demonstrated His love for me personally—and in every way that I had sought. Though my lack of vision, my lack of faithfulness, and my lack of love and trust in Him had robbed me so long of the peace and the joy and the rest that come from knowing and walking in God's love, these things had not caused Him to withhold His love from me. God, who is sovereign and who is the Almighty, did not grow weary with me; instead, like the loving husband and faithful friend who seeks to give us the desires of our hearts, He provided me with every requested proof of His love. But, like those disciples who walked along the Emmaus Road with the resurrected Jesus, I had not recognized who was already there with me. Not until I ceased my desperate attempts to earn or find His love did I come to know He had been walking and talking with me, demonstrating that love for me as we had journeyed together. I am glad that He answered me as He did. I am glad that He knows me so well that He knows how I will be best established in His love. I am glad that He loves me like that.

Because the world requires so much of us to be loved and accepted, some of us find it difficult to comprehend a love whose simple requirements are that we simply **be** and that we **believe**. Thus, when we desire to know God's love, we can get so caught up in trying to earn it and trying to get it that we miss it altogether. But how grateful I am and we all can be that God does not place such demands for performance on us. Instead, He stands ready to give us His love—just for the asking. To each of us He says, *"Here I am! I stand at the door and knock. If anyone hears my voice and opens the door, I will come in and eat with him, and he with me"* *(Revelations 3:20)*.

Yes, Jesus loves me! Yes, Jesus loves you, too! And He stands ready to pour out His love upon us all.

This is My commandment,
that you love one another as I have loved you.
(John 15:12 — NKJV)